ANGER IN / ANGER OUT
Your Roadmap to Understanding Anger

ANGER IN / ANGER OUT
Your Roadmap to Understanding Anger

Original Material © Copyright 2022
by Maria L. Vega and Breakthrough Innovative Group.
ISBN 978-1-7378050-0-7
Library of Congress Control Number: 2021917123

Published by Maria L. Vega and Breakthrough Innovative Group.
All rights reserved.

Printed in the United States of America
by Ingram Content Group. First Printing.

No portion of this work may be reproduced or transmitted in any form or by any means, electronic or mechanical, including photocopying and recording or by any information storage or retrieval system, without written permission from the author.

*NOTE: The assessments in this workbook are NOT diagnostic tools.
They are designed to be helpful tools only. Physical and mental health disorders
can only be diagnosed by qualified physicians and/or mental health professionals.*

*In most instances, pronouns in this book have been made gender-neutral intentionally,
with the use of they and them replacing the traditional use of he/she and him/her.*

Published in the United States, Canada, Europe
the United Kingdom, and Australia.

Address all queries to
Breakthrough Innovative Group.
info@breakthroughinnovative.com

ANGER IN / ANGER OUT

Your Roadmap to Understanding Anger

MARIA L. VEGA

About the Author

Maria L. Vega, CAMF, MPA, is dedicated to helping people attain greater understanding of themselves and their relationships with others. In her practice, she provides practical and innovative solutions designed to facilitate personal growth.

As a court-appointed anger management provider and corporate trainer, she brings extensive experience in fostering empowerment toward better relationships, improving job performance, helping to build stronger marriages, and encouraging a healthier lifestyle while also helping clients identify their short-term and long-term goals.

Ms. Vega holds a bachelor's degree in sociology and a master's degree in public administration. She is certified in anger management by Anderson & Anderson, APC.

Ms. Vega also has a broad range of experience in both the nonprofit and public sectors as a college instructor, social services manager, and director of career services for vocational colleges.

She heads the North Hollywood-based Breakthrough Innovative Group, where she exercises her professional expertise in the areas of stress management, public speaking, family services, communication, mediation, conflict resolution, company management, and much more.

Introduction

Congratulations! You are embarking on the first steps toward better understanding and managing your emotions. First, remember that you are not alone. Fear, happiness, sadness, surprise, and displeasure are emotions we all have felt regardless of our culture or life experience. Emotions are universal and do not always follow rules of logic. Even a strong emotion like anger is normal, natural, and often healthy.

I have built my company, Breakthrough Innovative Group, into a safe place where it is possible to acquire and utilize the tools you will need to look beyond your actions and recognize anger as a complex emotion. As a court-appointed anger management provider, workplace consultant, and corporate trainer with a background in public administration and sociology, I have seen emotions manifest themselves in many ways. I also know that there are real, achievable solutions.

In this book, *Anger In /Anger Out: Your Roadmap to Understanding Anger,* my primary objective is to provide the tools that lead to greater understanding and the peace of mind that each of us seeks and deserves. These tools will become guideposts designed to enable you to manage the stresses you may encounter in daily life at home, at work, in social settings, and in unexpected situations.

Each day, we encounter stressors. Most are minor and may even pass unnoticed, while other triggers require us to cope, adjust, or speak up.

According to recent surveys, 40% of U.S. workers admit to experiencing stress at their workplace, and 25% say that their job is the biggest source of stress.[1] For most of us, stress is actually a normal part of life. At times, stress can serve a useful purpose. It can motivate you to set goals, develop a plan to get that promotion you have been wanting, train for new job, join a gym, or run a marathon.

But if you don't learn how to manage your stress, it can become long-term and seriously interfere not only with your job, but with your family life, and your health. Later in this book, I will discuss more about the causes of stress and the different ways that you can manage it to improve your well-being.

Later on, we will also be discussing how life stresses, such as financial obligations, relationship problems, or a traumatic event such as the death of a loved one can trigger anger.

When stress leads to anger, learning to understand it can help identify its underlying causes. That is when we can truly begin to frame the solutions, bring positive energy into our lives, and advance toward dealing rationally with our stresses.

This book is intended to provide strategies for understanding and controlling the emotion of anger by identifying unmet needs, improving communication, and applying conflict resolution strategies in interpersonal relationships. This involves pinpointing problem areas and targeting specific needs. Among other strategies, you will receive information on how to recognize, assess, and de-escalate problematic situations.

Whether you are dealing with a workplace situation or struggling privately with emotions related to a personal relationship that you cannot control or understand, you are not alone.

Anger In / Anger Out is full of professionally developed yet practical information, guidelines, exercises, and strategies designed to identify problem areas, target specific needs, and implement practices to help individuals generally improve relationships with others. By learning to recognize what triggers your anger, i.e., identifying your needs and values, the door opens to allow more positive stimuli to enter, and anger will no longer be a damaging reaction.

You have arrived at what may be one of the most important crossroads in your life.

Each chapter of this book is devoted to a distinct subject area with exercises and worksheets designed that help illustrate how the information may apply to your unique circumstance. These exercises are not only instructive, but they can also be fun and promote greater self-awareness.

By the end of *Anger In / Anger Out*, you should be able to:

- Understand the connection between stress and anger.
- Identify unmet needs.
- Recognize the four styles of communication.
- Improve self-awareness and self-control.
- Understand your triggers.
- Increase your emotional intelligence.

CONTENTS

Chapter 1
What Everyone Should Know About Anger 1

Chapter 2
Triggers 13

Chapter 3
The Stress Formula: Understanding and Managing Stress 31

Chapter 4
Emotional Intelligence 53

Chapter 5
Nonverbal vs. Verbal Communication 65

Chapter 6
Developing Effective Communication 75

Chapter 7
Managing Relationships 91

Chapter 8
Managing Conflict 105

Chapter 9
Identifying Your Values 119

Chapter 10
Roadmap to Managing Your Emotions 129

Notes 141

> *Anger is your body's check-engine light.*
> – MARIA L. VEGA

CHAPTER 1

What Everyone Should Know About Anger

The first step on the journey toward understanding and managing anger is to recognize the warning signs. But to do that, you need to learn what to look for, and that takes education. In this case, education is not about ABCs and 123s or earning an advanced degree. This time you will be learning to recognize your needs, your triggers, your stressors, and more, all of which will help you on this transformative journey toward understanding and managing your emotions, including your anger.

First, it is important to understand that any time your needs are dismissed, ignored, or are not met, a feeling of anger can take hold. As a result, brain chemicals, including hormones such as cortisol, may be elevated and cause physical and emotional changes.

The physical signs of anger can include:

- **Fatigue**

- **Headache**

- **Increased blood pressure**

- **Muscle tension**

- **Tightening in the chest**

- **Heart palpitations**

You may be upset about something that happened that day and provoke an argument with someone who had nothing to do with what happened earlier. If you're in your car and someone drives too closely or moves into your lane unexpectedly, you might have thoughts of revenge and engage in road rage.

You can work toward achieving control of your anger by first recognizing the warning signs. Like the check-engine light on the dashboard of your car, a feeling of anger can indicate that something is bothering you, that a need is not being met or that something needs to be addressed.

With a car, ignoring the check engine light for too long can worsen the problem and lead to expensive repairs that might have otherwise been avoided. In the same way, ignoring or dismissing anger for too long can worsen a situation that could have otherwise been discussed and resolved.

Our emotions are substantially more complex than a car's engine, which is why it is important to be aware of what has led to an angry response and take steps to address it in a timely manner. In a car, the check engine light indicates that something is wrong. It might initially be an easy fix, but disregarding the warning light too long can make a minor problem become major and cost a lot more in the long run.

Anger works in the same way. It emerges when our needs are not being met, our values are being threatened, or we are trying to protect ourselves. Anger signals that something is not quite right. That's why ignoring your anger could cause it to grow into a much bigger problem that costs you more later . . . in your mental and emotional well-being, your relationships, and even your health.

Defining Anger

The term "anger" is applied generally to a feeling or emotion ranging from mild irritation to intense fury and rage. It is natural to react strongly in situations in which we feel threatened, we believe harm will come to us, or we believe that another person has unnecessarily wronged us.

We may react similarly when we believe that another person, such as a child or someone close to us, is being threatened or harmed. Such a response might even be considered an act of bravery.

> *Anger is a secondary emotion.*

When someone is angry, they feel hostile toward someone or something. It is primarily triggered by incidents that have caused or could cause harm. Although anger is situational, it is also influenced by a person's culture, personal triggers, and learned behaviors. Anger is connected to a person's basic survival instincts, i.e., fight-or-flight response.

Anger is a normal human emotion, and it can actually have some positive effects. When facing difficult circumstances, people can become more motivated through their anger; they can develop increased determination and persistence, with the result that they take continued action to promote positive change in their lives.

It can also act to preserve self-confidence and dignity and can spur someone to communicate circumstances and feelings that might not otherwise be brought into the open. Anger can prompt someone to persist in actions that can save a life (including one's own) rather than just giving up.

We're all aware that anger also can have negative effects, both personally and socially. When emotions are high, people tend to have less control over behavior, and the ability to think clearly can become impaired. Anger often incites an impulse toward aggression, so that if not managed effectively, it can motivate harmful behavior toward people or property.

According to the American Psychological Association's *Encyclopedia of Psychology*[2] such aggression often has negative consequences to relationships and lifestyle, and sometimes results in legal ramifications. An angry person does not always act wisely or with empathy and sometimes suffers physical consequences. When someone is excessively angry, they are not at their best.

The Four Styles of Communication (and Ways of Expressing Anger)

Another way of thinking about anger is in terms of its four types, or the four ways in which it is expressed:

1. **Aggressive**

    This is externalized behavior that can be verbal or physical, hostile, or nonverbal intimidation and can include threatening gestures and destruction of property.

2. **Passive-Aggressive**

    Those who are outwardly agreeable yet express anger indirectly are considered passive-aggressive. There is usually a disconnect between what passive-aggressive people say and what they do. For example, a person might agree and smile when you ask them to do something. They say, "Yes, of course! Happy to." But instead of doing what you asked, they express anger in a passive-aggressive way by not doing what was asked.

3. **Passive**

    Passive people can seem overly easygoing and often internalize anger. They may avoid conflict and submit to someone else's influence or fail to express honest feelings, thoughts, and beliefs. Internalizing anger or keeping feelings of anger inside can be just as harmful as externalizing anger.

4. **Assertive**

Expressing anger assertively means using words rather than taking negative action, speaking respectfully to the other person, and communicating without blaming.[3] It means talking about the feeling of anger directly without being argumentative. Expressing anger assertively can help individuals avoid conflict, maintain relationships, and open the door to compromise.

Education and Awareness

Learning about anger through education (such as studying the principles found in this workbook) and becoming more aware about how your own anger works will help reduce conflict in your relationships and help you avoid outbursts that may be caused by stress and/or miscommunication.

> *Anger management education:*
> *What we learn becomes part of who we are.*

Some of the first things we can learn are the most common myths about anger:

- *Anger is a bad emotion.* There is no such thing as a good or bad emotion; they are instinctual reactions, and we don't make conscious decisions to summon such emotions.

    In fact, some anger reactions are justified, such as the anger against observed injustice or violence. It is actually our *reaction* to our own anger that can be healthy or unhealthy.

- *You can't control your anger.* This myth is related to the previous myth. All of us have a natural "fight-or-flight" instinct that can make anger an overwhelming emotion. However, this instinct does not mean that you are a slave to your impulses.

Becoming aware of the dynamics of anger and making a conscious effort to apply specific tools in response to anger can help you regain control of your reactions.

- *Ignore it, and it will go away.* Denying that you feel an emotion can lead to indirect and usually more harmful impacts. Just as we discussed earlier about ignoring a "check engine light," ignore your anger, and it will be only temporarily shelved and likely find other ways of getting expressed.

  If we ignore our anger, we can sometimes unconsciously participate in something called "projection," which means we become angry at a person who has nothing to do with the real issue. That can also be considered misplaced anger. Anger can build up until we have an emotional outburst.

- *Time heals all wounds.* Studies show that there can be significant negative consequences to ignoring or suppressing your anger.[4]

- *Let it out, and you will feel better.* Venting anger does not necessarily result in dissipating angry feelings. Although a strong, outward expression of anger may provide a momentary sense of power, habitually exploding in anger can reinforce neurological pathways in the brain, harm your physical health, and ultimately destroy your relationships.

  Although venting can sometimes provide a release, expressing anger in verbally or physically aggressive ways is not the only way to "unleash" anger. Instead, you can learn how to identify your unmet needs and use assertive rather than aggressive ways to communicate your anger.

- *If I don't get angry, others will walk all over me.* In the short term, loudly expressing anger may yield results, but over time it pushes people away and reduces your credibility. Anger is not the only way a person can demonstrate that there are consequences to perceived violations. In fact, the most effective way of instilling discipline in others is to have a calm, non-emotional approach to dealing with boundary-breakers. Calm rationality can also communicate strength.

- *I cannot help it; I am an angry person.* Adopting this point of view can leave you at the mercy of your emotions.

What *is* anger, then? It is an emotional *response* to an internal or external threat, a personal violation or injustice, a feeling of powerlessness, or an unmet need. That response is often *Anger In / Anger Out*. In other words, you experience a strong, angry feeling (anger in), and you express it (anger out)—sometimes with negative results.

Your emotional responses—both the emotion you experience and how you express it—often depend on how you were raised and what you were taught growing up. Think about what you learned about your culture, gender, and values as you were growing up and how they influence who you are today and your current response to emotion. Write out your thoughts about each:

- **Culture** _____

_____

_____

_____

_____

- **Gender** _____

_____

_____

_____

_____

- **Values** _____

_____

_____

_____

_____

Anger: The Umbrella Emotion

Anger is easy to recognize because it is often expressed loudly and emotionally. It emerges when we feel vulnerable or are trying to protect ourselves. Yet experts in anger management sometimes refer to anger as an "umbrella emotion" or a "secondary" emotion, because it often covers other feelings. Anger may be hiding a primary emotion that you may be able to identify if you think a situation through.

Following is a list of some primary emotions:

Anxiety	Belonging	Betrayal	Blame	Disappointment
Disgust	Embarrassment	Empathy	Fear	Frustration
Guilt	Humiliation	Hurt	Jealousy	Loneliness
Overwhelmed	Regret	Sadness	Shame	Surprise
Vulnerability	Worry			

Think of a specific time you experienced anger; what were some of the primary emotions you may have been feeling? List two here, and briefly describe the situation.

1. _____

   _____

   _____

2. _____

   _____

   _____

What Is Internalized Anger?

While anger is a normal and even a healthy emotion and can result in effective change, holding anger inside is not healthy and can lead to sadness, anxiety, and depression.

If you find yourself overreacting to small irritations, screaming at other drivers on the road, or you become angry over insignificant circumstances (such as when dinner isn't ready), you could be suffering from internalized anger that has been building up inside of you for days, months, or possibly years. This is often referred to as "misplaced anger."

Misplaced anger is a defense mechanism and coping strategy in which a person denies their own thoughts and feelings and then redirects a response toward another person (or target) that is less threatening than the person or event that triggered the anger.

An example is someone who becomes angry with a spouse at home when the person who triggered the anger was their boss at work.[5]

Describe a time when you misplaced the emotion of anger:

_____

_____

_____

_____

Internalizing anger is a way of mismanaging it, and people who mismanage emotions can make life hard on others as well as on themselves. They can have trouble developing meaningful relationships and often place blame on others.

They sometimes read into the present what has happened to them in the past. They may have been hurt by parents, siblings, or others, and that hurt has turned to anger.

Mental health professionals have described the effects of internalized anger, which can include:[6]

- Addiction
- Apathy
- Anxiety
- Chronic illness
- Concentration difficulties
- Depression
- Heart problems
- High blood pressure
- Impulsiveness
- Impaired work performance
- Insomnia
- Self-destructive behaviors

What effects have you experienced from holding anger inside?

1. _____
2. _____
3. _____
4. _____
5. _____

Understanding why you feel angry, sad, lonely, or anxious is the first step to healthy relationships and greater contentment. Yet it is the emotions you want to experience most, such as happiness and hope, that contribute to a better sense of yourself and help you have more positive interactions with others.

When we have desirable emotions, such as a sense of accomplishment or compassion, the tension in our bodies increases and then is released in the form of laughter or excitement or feeling proud.

Reflect on some positive experiences in your life. Describe below what makes you feel happy:

_____

_____

_____

_____

At the same time, it is important to become aware of your other emotions, such as anxiety, resentment, and guilt, which sometimes build up inside and are stored rather than released. It is also important to understand what leads to anger, such as the various kinds of stress you experience, which then sometimes causes anger to explode outward, often with negative consequences.

Describe a challenging emotion you experience often:

_____

_____

_____

_____

In the pages of this workbook, you will learn even more about what causes anger and the tools available that will help you manage strong emotions. Having that awareness can contribute to a happier, more content, more satisfying life.

Take the following quiz to check your knowledge. What have you learned about anger so far?

CHECK YOUR ANGER UNDERSTANDING:

1. Anger is a bad emotion. — True / False
2. Anger can cause physiological changes. — True / False
3. Timid or shy people rarely experience anger. — True / False
4. It is normal and natural to feel angry occasionally. — True / False
5. Anger is a secondary emotion — True / False
6. Anger is almost always caused by stress. — True / False

> *Identifying your needs will improve your life.*
> – MARIA L. VEGA

CHAPTER 2
Triggers

Sometimes you may read a map incorrectly. Or even if you do read it correctly, you might miss a landmark or a sign that would have enabled you to take the correct turn you needed to reach your destination. Similarly, you may read your emotions incorrectly. It is tempting to attribute many feelings to anger, but this may not always be the case. Understanding why you are feeling anxious, annoyed, frustrated, or insulted is a key to gaining control of your emotions.

The events that trigger an emotion and the ways in which you express your feelings can vary greatly. To gain control of your emotions, specifically your anger, it helps to understand why you are feeling that emotion and what caused your emotional reaction in the first place.

Anger can be triggered by stress, by a perceived threat of harm, by unmet needs (basic and otherwise), by feelings of powerlessness, and even by ignoring or actively dismissing your anger. Let's learn about how all of that works.

Triggers, Unmet Needs, and Stressors – The Causes of Anger

Anger is often caused by specific triggers, unmet needs, and stressors in our lives. But there are differences between the three.

A *trigger* is a stimulus—either internally or from somewhere in your surrounding environment—that causes an immediate, often unexpected and uncontrollable, reaction. It is often a response to an earlier trauma and sometimes results in a panic attack. Think of a solider who has come back from war who has no control over his emotional and physical response—fear, anxiety, sweating, rapid breathing—upon hearing the boom of fireworks that immediately calls up memories of the gunshots and bombs of warfare.

Identify two current or potential triggers in your life:

1. _____

2. _____

A *stressor* is often not as immediate. It can be, but many times it is a longer-term circumstance in your environment that causes a stress response. A stressor can be anything from a police officer stopping you for a traffic violation (an immediate stressor) to significant life changes, such as getting married, moving, or becoming a parent, to long-term stressors such as chronic illness or difficult circumstances at work over which you may have no control.[7]

A stressor may be a threat of (or actual) loss to your body, property, self-esteem, values, or control. You can also be triggered by a stressor when thoughts about its impact on your well-being lead to a hostile response.

Stressors are often related to work, family, health, and money.

Identify two current or potential stressors in your life:

1. _____

2. _____

An *unmet need* is something that is lacking in your life. Unmet needs can be physical, emotional, financial, or even spiritual. Having an unmet need can sometimes be either a trigger or a stressor that contributes to an angry response.

Identify two current unmet needs in your life:

1. _____

2. _____

The truth is that we rarely ever become angry for the reasons we think. Anger can be related to your past, your present, and/or your future. Remembering a past event, experience, or person can trigger anger. A reaction to a real or perceived violation can lead to immediate anger. Thoughts of an imagined or anticipated violation can also become the root of anger.

Fear is a natural response to threats of violence or physical or verbal abuse and can lead to anger. Annoyance and life's minor irritations can also cause anger to build over time. Similarly, disappointment due to the perceived failure to meet a goal or expectation may stir up feelings of helplessness, which can lead to an angry response. Resentment can emerge when someone feels rejected, offended, or hurt.

It is important to consider the dynamics of anger. Do you know the typical circumstances that lead to an angry response?

An angry response can occur when you are **stressed**, and your body resources are down. Write down two examples of when stress has depleted your body's resources (reduced energy level, illness, injury, etc.):

1. _____

2. _____

An angry response can occur when traumas and underlying **disappointments** from the past surface and trigger anger. Write down two examples of when you have experienced disappointment:

1. _____

2. _____

An angry response can occur when a current event brings up an old, **unresolved incident**. Write down two examples of unresolved incidents that have triggered your anger:

1. _____

2. _____

Fight or Flight

Another way of understanding the way that strong emotions, such as anger, can be triggered is to study how certain physical systems work in the human body. It is believed that there is an evolutionary component to anger, that it is rooted in how human behavior has changed over time. While human behavior has adapted to changes in the environment, one of the driving forces of behavior is still based in the brain: the *fight-or-flight* or *acute stress response*, which is a psychological term that describes how some people react when under stress.

The fight-or-flight response is often characterized by an **increased heart rate, faster breathing, feeling pressure in your chest**, and **heightened sensitivity to sights and sounds**. All of this occurs as the body prepares to fight or to run in reaction to a perceived threat in the environment.

The fight-or-flight theory, formulated in the 1920s by physiologist Walter Cannon, describes how people react to a perceived threat.[8] When faced with something that can harm us, we either aggress (fight) or withdraw (flight). It is believed that this reaction is part of the survival instinct inside each of us.

When we are faced with a threat, the fight-or-flight instinct causes our bodies to release the following stress hormones from the adrenal glands, which sit above the kidneys. These chemicals take us into a state of alertness and action and can even slow our digestion:

1. Adrenaline – increases energy, heart rate, muscle contraction, and breathing.

2. Noradrenaline – increases the strength of skeletal muscle contraction and the rate and strength of the contraction of the heart.

3. Cortisol – increases glucose (nutrition/fuel) levels available for muscles to use.

Understanding the fight-or-flight instinct can help us understand the dynamics of our anger response. First, the fight-or-flight response is natural. Being angry is neither moral nor immoral. In this case, anger is a response to a threat of harm, and it doesn't matter whether that harm is physical or emotional.

Additionally, when we become angry, our rational self is overruled by our basic survival instinct, and we suddenly feel we must take immediate action. Because of the tendency to act on impulse, it becomes even more important to stay in control, otherwise this instinct can result in:

- **Aggressiveness**

- **Overreactivity**

- **Hypervigilance**

All of these responses are contrary to rational and deliberate responses. Self-awareness and control are needed so that the fight-or-flight instinct does not overpower us.

The Limbic System

Emotional functions are largely housed in the limbic system, which are brain structures located on both sides of the thalamus immediately beneath the medial temporal lobe of the cerebrum. The limbic system supports a variety of functions,

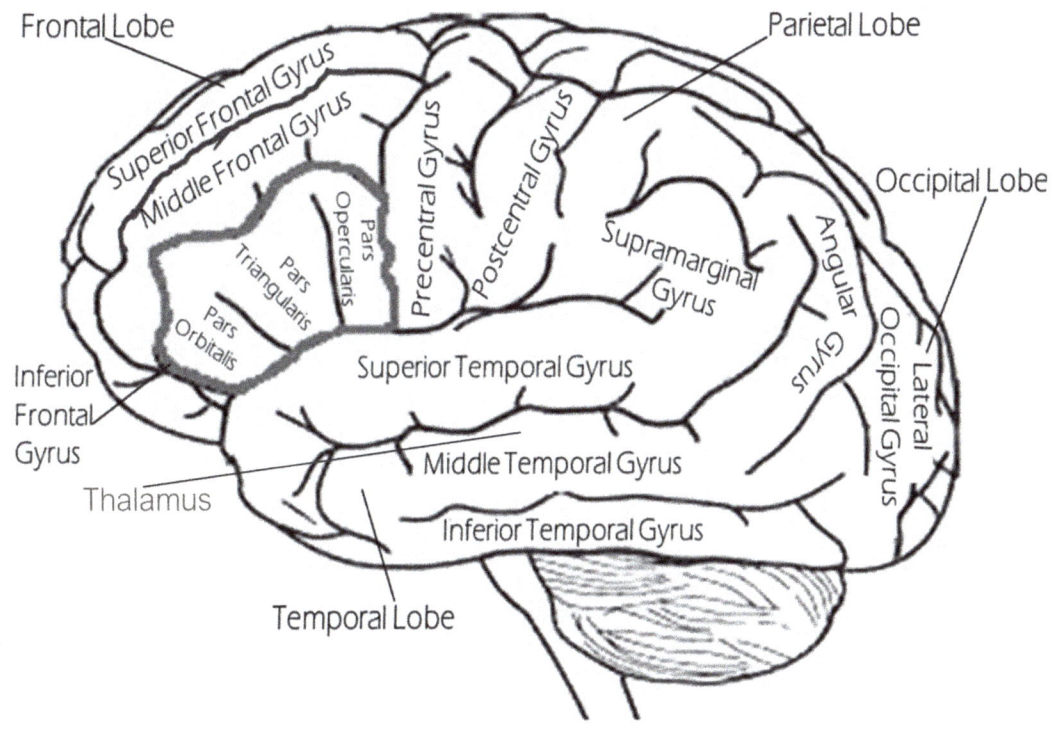

including emotion, behavior, long-term memory, and olfaction (sense of smell) and aids in the formation of memories.

Anger or fear can be triggered when a situation mirrors a situation from the past, through the experience of similar feelings, words, or senses (such as hearing, smell, or touch). These experiences activate the limbic system.

How does the activation of this system relate to your experience of anger? Much like what happens when you experience fear in response to a threat, anger also starts with stimulation of the limbic system.[9]

Research indicates that the limbic system acts something like a bridge between your emotions (the psychological) and the responses taking place in your body (the physiological), such as the fight-or-flight mechanism, that are often triggered by fear or anger.

When you feel threatened or angry, your brain activates the limbic system, which prompts the release of hormones, some of which raise your blood pressure, respiration, and heart rate. For example, cortisol, which is produced by the adrenal glands, is your body's main stress hormone and works to control your mood,

motivation, and fear. Those who have problems controlling anger may have higher levels of this stress hormone.

Your body needs this system as a form of self-protection when there are real threats to your safety and well-being, though in the long term, the over-release of some hormones can cause physiological damage.[10] According to the Mayo Clinic, this damage can include:

- Anxiety.

- Depression.

- Digestion problems.

- Headaches.

- Memory and concentration impairment.

- Muscle pain and tension.

- High blood pressure, heart disease, heart attack, and stroke.

- Sleep problems.

- Weight gain.[11]

Yet there is more to it than fear and anger. As an umbrella emotion, anger can sometimes cover up feelings of rejection, embarrassment, fear, insecurity, sadness, shame, hurt, safety, loneliness, or betrayal.

Physical expressions of these emotions vary greatly. Feeling that your "blood is boiling," sweating, shaking, having a headache or an upset stomach—all can be part of an anger response.

Another example is gastrointestinal disorders, which often have a direct link to strong emotions; a chronically angry person secretes more enzymes and hydrochloric acid, eventually breaking down the stomach membrane that can result in ulcers.

Once these physiological responses are activated, behavioral responses can include anything from attacking someone to getting defensive to walking away.

At the same time, it is important to remember that each emotion serves an essential function, and that there is no such thing as a good or bad emotion. Below is a list of some constructive purposes for our emotions:

> **WHEN EMOTIONS ARE GOOD FOR YOU . . .**
>
> **Anger** – Protects, creates, and asserts boundaries.
>
> **Fear** – Provides safety.
>
> **Happiness** – Instills a feeling of satisfaction.
>
> **Sadness** – Allows us to grieve.
>
> **Guilt** – Leads to correction and self-respect.
>
> **Shame** – Needed for approval and social acceptance.
>
> **Hurt** – Important for healing.
>
> **Loneliness** – Forces us to seek social connection and relationships.

Unmet Basic Needs

Often when someone feels a strong emotion, such as anger, sadness, frustration, or even being overwhelmed, it's because a need is not being met. A child acting out at school may have an unmet need at home. A person who feels overwhelmed may need to set aside time to relax. A person who experiences sudden anger may feel unsafe, meaning there is an unmet need for safety.

Sometimes strong emotions can be triggered when life's basic needs are not being met. What are our basic human needs?

- Need to survive—food, safety, shelter.

- Need for connection—fulfilled by loving, sharing, and cooperating with others.

- Need for control or power over one's life—fulfilled by having/making choices in life.

- Need for fun—fulfilled by laughing and playing.

- Need for meaning in life—fulfilled by achieving and being recognized and respected.

Other Needs

Sometimes anger can be the result of the frustration we feel when other needs, desires, and goals are not being addressed. An unmet need can also sometimes grow into overwhelming feelings of sadness or helplessness.

Here are a few examples. Add two more examples of your own needs to the list:

1. The need to feel loved.

2. The need to be understood.

3. The need for others to be honest with me.

4. The need to be respected.

5. The need for emotional support.

6. The need for security.

7. _____

8. _____

> *Here are a few other common needs:* **affection, appreciation, being heard, being valued, connection, creativity, empathy, freedom, imagination, movement, love, presence, recognition, relaxation, respect, safety, shared responsibility, touch.**

Underlying feelings of fear, hurt, sadness, or shame can be the underlying result of unmet needs and can emerge as anger. It is important, therefore, to delve beneath the surface and identify unmet needs in order to pinpoint the cause of anger rather than misplace anger onto the person or persons involved in a conflict.

Noticing and naming your feelings can help you identify subtle differences between different types of emotions and help you understand better why you react the way you do. Identifying your needs can be an eye-opening experience that can also help you improve your interpersonal relationships.

By identifying unmet needs, working toward greater understanding of emotions, and learning how to communicate effectively, you can begin to achieve emotional growth.

> *Anger can be an indicator to yourself that your needs are not being met.*

Needs in Personal Relationships

In personal relationships, it is not unusual for unmet needs to build over time. Learning to recognize those unmet needs, both in yourself and in your partner, and then being able to listen to what your partner needs and communicate your own needs assertively, will contribute to a more effective, satisfying relationship.

You may not always be able to recognize in someone else when that person's need is not being met, so you may need to ask on occasion.

When you do need to show empathy to your partner, sometimes it is best to simply be with that person during what is happening at the present moment, i.e., recognizing the person's current emotional state.

Gently saying things like, "This is tough, isn't it?" or "I can really feel how hard this is for you" may be the most effective starting point.

List five common needs that occur in your close relationships (Example: *"I would like to experience a feeling of trust in my relationship"*):

NEEDS IN A PERSONAL RELATIONSHIP

1. _____
2. _____
3. _____
4. _____
5. _____

Additionally, in the workplace, unmet needs can lead to stress and frustration. Below, identify several of your needs in the workplace. (Example: *I need autonomy, creativity, and growth.*):

NEEDS IN THE WORKPLACE

1. _____
2. _____
3. _____
4. _____
5. _____

Feeling Powerless

What are some other circumstances that trigger anger? In addition to being threatened or attacked, you might experience anger if you feel powerless, frustrated, disrespected, invalidated, or when you feel you are being treated unfairly.[12]

Anger often begins with a sense of helplessness. Someone who feels helpless may personalize the experience, wondering "Why is this being done to me?" They may believe that something is unfair and may feel:

- Threatened

- Vulnerable

- Exposed

- Ashamed

- Victimized

- Violated

- Inadequate

Yet just because you feel powerless or helpless doesn't mean you actually are. In other words, when your fear is "talking," you don't have to listen.

There are specific actions you can take to overcome feelings of helplessness:

- Make a list of your skills and strengths, so you will be reminded of your capabilities.

- Pay closer attention to your thoughts—negative thoughts can lead to feelings of hopelessness and helplessness—and work at replacing them with more positive thinking.

- Identify a small action you can take that will move you toward a specific goal that will improve your current situation.

- Refocus—rather than emphasizing the problem, consider possible solutions.[13]

Pretending You're Not Angry

Ignoring your feelings can turn your anger into a stressor that contributes to even more anger or other harmful consequences. Pretending you're not angry is not a solution nor is believing that you can handle things alone. Some common results of suppressing anger include:

- *Depression* – You may begin to lose interest in things you once enjoyed such as hobbies, work, friends, or sex. Keeping your feelings bottled up may lead to more serious conditions.

- *Problems at Work* – Angry outbursts on the job can lead to a negative impression of you among coworkers, poor decision-making, and poor judgment, negatively impacting your career.

- *Substance Abuse* – Using alcohol or other drugs to dull strong feelings usually results in more anger and leads to other problems. Substance use can cause you to forget about the negative consequences of an angry outburst.

- *Health Problems* – Giving up control of your emotions can affect your physical health in the form of headaches, sleep problems, digestive ailments, high blood pressure, and cardiovascular disease.

- *Damaged Relationships* – Failure to control anger can lead to criticizing, insulting, or threatening those close to you. In turn, they may respond with anger or resentment, which could keep you from resolving the situation by telling your loved ones how you really feel.

- *Low Self-Esteem* – The feeling that you are not able to understand or manage your anger can cause you to feel badly about yourself and/or have little control over what happens.

Learning to Recognize Your Anger

Symptoms of repressed anger include hypersensitivity, inflexibility, fear of rejection, conflict, feelings of abandonment, overachieving, and over-control. Anger is often expressed as a momentary release, even an emotional explosion, but this does not reduce overall stress. Defusing anger reduces tension and stress momentarily but does not address the cause of anger.

Anger often masks other emotions, such as sadness, helplessness, and fear. Additionally, what is perceived as sadness, chronic fatigue, rationalization, blame, and cynicism can also conceal underlying feelings of anger.

> *Education never ends. Neither do emotions.*

Psychological conditions such as depression, unresolved trauma, substance abuse, or brain injury can appear outwardly as anger. Tense muscles, tight fists, clenched jaw, sweaty palms, upset stomach, a loud or mean voice are among the signs that you are close to becoming angry.

Acknowledge your responsibility for your own emotions and actions; however, by taking note of these signs, you will begin to learn to control your anger before it takes control of you.

Can you identify the current cause(s) of your anger?

_____

_____

_____

_____

Self-Awareness

Describe the bodily symptoms or changes in behavior you experience when you're angry:

_____

_____

_____

_____

Additionally, when anger is directed toward you, it is just as important to be able to recognize the signs of anger in others.

It helps to remember that "Hurt people hurt people."[14]

Do not take it personally. Other people's anger is their responsibility, not yours. When confronted by someone who is angry, try modeling calmness. Talk about it rather than ignore it. Listen openly and show understanding. Offer reassurance.

Describe a time when someone got angry at you and how you handled it:

_____

_____

_____

_____

You can learn to better understand your anger and its causes by closer self-examination. Start by thinking about when you have become angry in the recent past.

Ask yourself these questions (answer honestly and write down one or two examples):

- Do I overreact to minor annoyances? Is my level of anger or my reaction out of proportion to the trigger?

_____

_____

_____

_____

- Am I really angry with the person who triggered my response? Or am I directing my anger to the wrong person?

  _____

  _____

  _____

  _____

- Do I deal with anger by taking things personally?

  _____

  _____

  _____

- Do I always react with anger in certain situations?

  _____

  _____

  _____

  _____

- Am I afraid of losing control and in response try to change that by expressing anger or internalizing it?

_____

_____

_____

_____

Now that you have learned what can trigger anger, take a few moments to consider your own triggers. Complete the following exercise:

WHAT TRIGGERS YOUR ANGER?

Think about (a) the circumstances that trigger your anger and (b) what in your past may have caused you to react the way you did. Make a list.

TRIGGER:	ROOT OR CAUSE:
1. _____	_____
2. _____	_____
3. _____	_____
4. _____	_____

> *ANGER – a healthy emotion
> mismanaged by misunderstanding.*
> – MARIA L. VEGA

CHAPTER 3
The Stress Formula: Understanding and Managing Stress

No one needs to tell you that life is dynamic and constantly changing. Yet this simple fact of life creates emotional, mental, and physical stress, which in turn can affect all aspects of your life.

It's not possible to avoid stress entirely. Instead, one trick to happier, more successful relationships is to learn how to manage stress and navigate successfully through the situations that cause it. If handled correctly, it is often the most stressful situations in life that bring out our best.

When we are working our way along the road toward managing our emotions and our stress, there is a key that will unlock the door and allow us to successfully navigate difficult circumstances (that cause stress) and feelings (such as anger). That key is *education*.

But just like you have to practice doing arithmetic problems when you are learning, let's say algebra or geometry, you also must practice the techniques and strategies that will help you understand and manage both stress and anger.

The good news is that you can learn and practice strategies that work to manage the inevitable pressures that comes with being a human being in a stressful world.[15]

Stress is a physical, mental, or emotional state that causes significant tension in the body. In simpler terms, it is the body's natural reaction to change, generally requiring a certain adjustment or response. According to a recent study, about 25%

of Americans say they are dealing with high levels of stress, while another 50% claim they have moderate stress.[16]

According to WebMD, "While some day-to-day stress is normal and can even be good if it motivates you, chronic, overwhelming stress can have a negative impact on your physical, mental, and emotional well-being."[17]

We developed the Stress Formula as a tool to help simplify decision-making and remove the emotion that often drives and complicates stressful situations. In short, the Stress Formula enables you to focus on possible solutions and de-escalate a problem rather than amplify it to the point where it leads to an angry response.

Demands and Resources

What is the Stress Formula?

$$\textbf{Demand + Resources = Root Cause}$$

Identifying the Demand at hand + Identifying what Resources are available to you to meet that demand = Allows you to identify the Root Cause of your stress.

In other words, what causes stress is a lack of resources to meet a demand.

You can use this formula to recognize exactly what is causing your stress.

Here's an example: You have a monthly mortgage payment of $_____ (demand) but your monthly income only allows you to apply $_____ (resource) toward the mortgage. The dilemma of how to make up the $_____ shortfall is the problem that causes you stress. You find yourself blaming your job or the high mortgage—factors that you cannot immediately change.

Complete the following self-assessment by thinking about situations in your own life. What are some current demands on your time, energy, relationships, finances, or work? Are there sufficient resources available to meet each demand?

Current Demand	Resources Available
1.	
2.	
3.	
4.	
5.	
6.	
7.	

Stress is both a natural response and an outcome, and it is often both physical and psychological. Depending on whether the stressor is negative or positive, adrenalin may surge, and blood pressure may rise. This is the body's reaction as it tries to return the body's systems to normal levels.

While elevated adrenalin might have been useful in helping prehistoric humans run away from danger, today's stressors are quite different, and the residual effects of prolonged elevation of adrenalin or cortisol can sometimes be harmful.

Yet the stress is real. By identifying the root cause of your dilemma—in the example, the monthly shortfall in the mortgage payment—the need is identified, and the impulse to blame other factors or other people is avoided.

By applying the formula, instead of allowing frustration to build that can develop into misdirected anger, you can focus your energies on seeking a solution.

Internal and External Stress

Think of your body as a finely tuned instrument that does not like surprises. Any sudden change that affects your emotions can cause stress, and that can result in

negative impacts. When stress remains unresolved, it can erupt as anger and take a toll on your physical health. Stress can raise blood pressure, damage relationships, lead to self-destructive habits, and cause excessive levels of anger that may become more difficult to control over time.

There are two types of stressors: internal and external.

Internal stressors are those stress triggers that are within each person. These can range from feeling irritable to feeling tired or unappreciated. Negative thoughts and automatic thinking are forms of internal stressors.

Examples include putting pressure on yourself to be perfect, having unrealistic expectations, or having a consistently running dialogue of negative self-talk (negative thoughts).

You could even consider being fired as an internal stressor, because being fired is often based on choices an employee makes to violate a rule on the job or to refuse to recognize that a job is not a good fit.

Give an example of internal stress in your life—either something that is currently happening or something that happened in the past:

_____

_____

_____

_____

_____

When thinking about internal stressors, it's important to understand that everyone feels irritable at times. Irritation can be a step toward anger and can tell you that something is wrong.

Additionally, anxiety occurs when you feel that you can't control an outcome. Irritation and anxiety are called "swing emotions," because they can either improve or agitate your state of mind. When not addressed, these emotions can reinforce negative thoughts and feelings.

One way of addressing these feelings is to work at slowing down your thoughts. Actions you can take to quiet your mind include deep breathing, exercise, listening to music, going outdoors, hanging out with a favorite pet, creative activities (artwork, knitting, crafting, woodworking), gardening, and even watching fish swim in an aquarium.[18]

External stressors relate to your environment. They can involve anything from loud, annoying alarm clocks to crowded elevators to caring for a sick loved one, and can even include positive events, such as gaining recognition for an achievement.

External stressors are often beyond our control.

Examples of external stressors include being laid off from work, a demanding boss, morning gridlock, or relationship problems with a family member or friend. (By contrast, internal stressors are primarily related to your thoughts and behaviors, based on the choices you make each day.)

Give an example of an external stressor in your life that is currently happening or happened in the past.

_____

_____

_____

_____

_____

External stressors can often be a source of frustration. You can better manage stress from external stressors by practicing adaptability and focusing on controlling what you can.

Becoming aware of which of your stressors are internal and which are external will help you on your journey toward better understanding anger.

Take some time to think about and identify some internal and external stressors in your life and list them below:

Internal Stressors	External Stressors
1.	1.
2.	2.
3.	3.
4.	4.
5.	5.

Short-Term and Long-Term Stress

Short-term stress, sometimes also called acute stress, may be temporary, but can still influence how you react. Short-term stress may happen over minutes, hours, or even a few days.

Examples of short-term stress include moving, recovering from a minor injury or illness, or being stuck in a traffic jam on the way to work. Examples of the acute type of short-term stress are being in a car accident or experiencing some kind of trauma.

Short-term stress may activate the body's fight-or-flight response. A person's heart races, breathing becomes faster, muscles tense, and the person under stress may start to sweat. The body usually recovers quickly. Milder forms of short-term stress can sometimes be positive; for example, it may provide additional energy and motivation when you are planning a wedding or starting a new job.

Long-term stress, sometimes known as chronic stress, affects your life over an extended period of time, sometimes weeks, months, or years. Examples of long-term stress include a chronic illness, a toxic work environment, or a difficult relationship with a spouse or partner. Long-term stress can sometimes develop into health problems, such as high blood pressure, obesity, and depression. It can cause you to lose sleep or feel overwhelmed, worried, or unmotivated.

It is important to recognize both kinds of stress in your life so that you can develop strategies to improve how you manage it. In the chart below, list some your own short-term and long-term stressors:

Short-Term Stressors	Long-Term Stressors
1.	1.
2.	2.
3.	3.
4.	4.
5.	5.

Understanding Stress in the Workplace

It's also helpful to think specifically about what could be causing you stress in your workplace. Try the following exercise:

REASONS FOR WORKPLACE STRESS

(*Example: Heavy workload, working long hours.*)
List other causes of stress on your job:

1. _____

2. _____

3. _____

4. _____

5. _____

Once you have determined what is causing you stress in the workplace, you can then brainstorm ways in which you can address it.

Some strategies for coping with workplace stress include:

1. Take breaks.
2. Exercise.
3. Get plenty of rest/sleep.
4. Establish boundaries.
5. Take time to recharge.
6. When appropriate, speak to your supervisor.[19]

Tracking Your Stress

Remember that we all have different needs. How we manage stress is unique and personal to each of us. Daily life stressors can often be overwhelming and may make you feel like withdrawing from family and friends and isolating yourself.

Keeping a journal can assist you in measuring your stress and ultimately help you develop a plan of action to manage it.

Instructions: *Below is a sample of a journal. Write down how you are feeling and, most important, how you are dealing or not dealing with the stressor(s).*

Date	Stress Cause	Physical Feeling	Emotional Reaction	Behavior	Internal/ External

Developing a Plan of Action for Managing Stress

There are many ways of managing your stress, but the key word in accomplishing stress management is "action." Setting goals and then creating a plan for achieving those goals works just as well for diminishing and responding well to stress as it does for anything else.

Outlined in this workbook are multiple ways for reducing and working toward eliminating the kinds of stress over which you have some control. These stress management techniques include:

- Reducing your to-do list.
- Avoiding stressful people and situations as much as possible.
- Avoiding "hot" topics.
- Seeking to regain control where you can.
- Applying specific relaxation techniques.
- Taking a pause.
- Eliminating unhealthy coping strategies.

These specific techniques are explained in the following sections. At the end of this chapter is an additional list of tips for reducing stress that you can try. Use those that best work for you.

Reduce Your To-Do List

Having too many things to do and too little time to do them is stressful. While it is not always possible to eliminate all the tasks that demand your attention, making small changes can simplify your life and help reduce stress.

Pare down your "to do" list by separating the tasks into two categories—those tasks that are *necessary* and those that are *unnecessary*. Putting tasks onto one of these lists helps you to identify those that are low-priority and not urgent. Try doing this in the following exercise:

Instructions: *Start by making two lists. In one list, write down the things that must be done, such as "call my client" or "pick up the kids from school." In another list, write down those tasks that may be unnecessary, such as "alphabetize my bookshelf."*

To Do List: Necessary	To Do List: Unnecessary

Avoid Stressful People and Situations

The chart below can assist you in identifying individuals or situations that cause your stress. Think about what happens when someone makes you feel like escaping, such as the person who insists on sharing the latest gossip or the coworker who constantly complains.

Person or Situation	Describe

Avoid Hot Topics

Most people will agree that bringing up certain topics, such as politics, religion, and family issues, can lead to arguments. Think about what should be avoided in conversations with family, friends, and coworkers. Describe them below.

1. _____
2. _____
3. _____
4. _____
5. _____

Seek to Regain Control

There are several specific techniques you can use to regain control of a stressful situation or stressful thoughts. Try any one (or more) of the following:

1. Apply the Stress Formula using the Demand/Resource analysis.

2. Determine whether your stress is the result of external or internal factors.

3. Take note of your body's signals. This may the first sign that you are experiencing stress.

4. Implement a personal de-escalation plan. Here are a few suggestions:

    - Take a different route to work.
    - Listen to music.
    - Light a candle.
    - Exercise.
    - Talk to a friend.

5. Apply self-awareness techniques. How much stress do you think you are currently under? Check the warning signs. Consider the ways you can

eliminate some of the stress that could cause you physical, emotional, or behavioral difficulties as well as what might work to help you decompress.

Identify four things that work to calm you down (for example: *deep breathing*):

1. _____

2. _____

3. _____

4. _____

Practice Relaxation

When you are under stress, the body's muscles tighten up and breathing becomes rapid and shallow. An effective way to stop this response to stress is to breathe slowly and deeply. Deep breathing sometimes seem unnatural, especially to adults, but can help reverse the effects of stress.

You can be sitting, standing, or lying down. Begin by breathing in through your nostrils. Count to five and silently say the word "in." Let your lower abdomen fill with air. Then count to five, silently saying "out" as you blow the air out. With practice, you will be able to count slowly to ten or higher.

You can increase your relaxation if, as you're practicing your deep breathing, you imagine you are walking along the ocean or through a field of flowers.

Deep breathing can allow held-in emotions such as anger to come to the surface. It also helps you let go of tension, can relieve headaches, backaches, stomach aches, and sleeplessness.

Stop What You're Doing

Whenever you start to feel that your anger warning signs are developing and you begin to think angry thoughts, tell yourself to stop. Try to calm down so you can think more clearly. If you can walk away for a few moments, that may be beneficial.

Try counting to 10 or 100. It may seem like old-fashioned advice, but it works! Scientifically, counting allows for your adrenalin, pulse, and heart rate to return to their normal state, and it works even better if you take deep breaths as you count.[20]

If you're angry with your partner or a family member, tell them that you need to take a time-out, then go to a safe place. Once you have the emotion of anger under control, go back and face the situation.

Eliminating Unhealthy Coping Strategies

Internalized anger and passive aggressive behavior can result in unresolved stress that often erupts as unacceptable behavior, such as aggression, and can even cause illness. Learn healthier ways to manage stress by changing your situation or your reaction to the situation.

Why bother? Because unhealthy stress-coping strategies such as smoking, excessive alcohol consumption, overeating or restricting food, electronic overload, social isolation, prescription or illegal drug use, procrastination, blaming others, and excessive sleeping can cause long-term harm.

Instructions: *Identify any unhealthy coping strategies you may have. In the column next to the negative strategy, write a healthy coping strategy you could implement instead.*

Unhealthy Coping Strategy	Healthy Strategy Option

More About Stress

Stress is how the brain and body respond to the demands of life.[21] Any type of challenge—such as your performance at work or school, a significant life change, or a traumatic event—can be stressful.

Stress can affect your health. It is important to pay attention to how you deal with minor and major stressors, so you know when to seek help. It can help to keep the following aspects of stress in mind:

- **Stress Affects Everyone**

    Everyone experiences stress from time to time. There are different types of stress—all of which carry physical and mental health risks.
    A stressor may be a one-time or short-term occurrence, or it can happen repeatedly over a long time. Some people may cope with stress more effectively and recover from stressful events more quickly than others.

What are your newly identified coping mechanisms for stress?

_____

_____

_____

_____

_____

- **Not All Stress Is Bad**

    In a dangerous situation, stress signals the body to prepare to face a threat or flee to safety. In non-life-threatening situations, stress can motivate people, such as when they need to take a test or interview for a new job.

    Describe a time when you used stress to inspire or motivate you:

    _____

    _____

    _____

    _____

- **Long-term Stress Can Harm Your Health**

    Over time, continued strain on your body from stress may contribute to serious health problems, such as heart disease, high blood pressure, diabetes, and other illnesses, including mental health disorders such as depression or anxiety.

Has your health or emotional well-being been impacted by stress? In what way(s)?

_____

_____

_____

_____

_____

More Tips for Managing Stress

Here are some additional tips that may help you cope better with stress:

Strengthen your relationships:

- Stay connected. You are not alone. Keep in touch with people who can provide emotional support and practical help.

- Whenever possible, avoid people or situations that you know will cause you stress.

- Express your feelings instead of keeping them inside.

- Be willing to compromise.

- Talk to your health care provider or other health professional.

Adjust your personal habits:

- Avoid excessive alcohol, caffeine, fats, sugar, and smoking.

- Exercise regularly. Just thirty minutes per day of walking can help boost your mood and improve your health. (Check with your doctor first.)

Develop self-management techniques:

- Managing stress often starts with asserting yourself. Pause before you say yes. Learn when to say no. It's okay to say no.

- Take control of your environment (turn off the news, avoid traffic, etc.).

- Set goals and priorities.

- Manage your time more efficiently.

Improve your attitudes:

- View stressful situations with a more positive perspective.

- Focus on the positive. Appreciate the good things in your life.

- Look at the big picture. Will this problem matter in a month?

- Adjust your standards. Being completely perfect isn't possible.

- Volunteer your time to an organization (or someone) you believe in. Giving service often helps keep personal circumstances in perspective.

Take a break from your routines:

- Take time to relax each day.

- Try a relaxing activity.

- Get away for the weekend.

> *Check your current level of stress on the next page.*

EXERCISE – CHAPTER 3

CHECK YOUR STRESS LEVEL

There are many ways to assess your stress level. One is to consider the physical effects of stress. Another is to measure how stress affects you mentally and emotionally. A third is to determine how many outside stressors (life changes) have occurred in your life recently.[22]

The following checklists can serve as ways to judge your current level of stress. Are you experiencing several physical symptoms of stress? Are those combined with mental and emotional symptoms? Have you had one or more significant life changes occur recently? If so, you may be experiencing more stress than you realize.

LIFE CHANGES THAT CONTRIBUTE TO STRESS

<u>Instructions</u>: *Place a checkmark next to any item you have experienced in the past year:*

	Beginning or ending school		Foreclosure		Sexual challenges
	Change in spouse's employment		Gain or loss of income		Significant business change
	Change in work responsibilities		Loved one's health challenges		Significant illness or injury
	Death of a friend or family member		Marriage		Spousal arguments
	Difficult in-law relationship		Moving		Spousal separation or reconciliation
	Divorce		New family member		Termination of employment
	Empty nest		New job		Other significant life change
	Expectant parenthood		New mortgage or refinance		
	Extraordinary personal success		Retirement		

49

PHYSICAL EFFECTS OF STRESS

<u>Instructions</u>: *Place a checkmark next to any persistent physical symptom of stress you have experienced in the past year:*

	Bleeding / infected gums		Muscle tension
	Difficulty breathing		Pain (stomach, muscles, chest, head)
	Difficulty with concentration or memory		Perspiration without exertion
	Digestive problems		Rapid heartbeat without exertion
	Dryness of the mouth		Self-mutilation
	Frequent colds or other illnesses		Shakiness in legs
	Headaches		Sleep disturbance
	High blood pressure		Unexplained chronic fatigue
	Impotence (males)		Weight gain or loss
	Irregular periods (females)		Other frequent physical symptoms

Please note that not all of these physical symptoms may be attributable solely to stress. See your doctor to determine whether there is another underlying physical cause for your symptoms.

MENTAL AND EMOTIONAL EFFECTS OF STRESS

Instructions: *Place a checkmark next to any ongoing mental or emotional symptoms of stress you have experienced in the past year:*

	Anxiety		Feeling powerless
	Constantly worrying		Feeling time pressured/rushed
	Depression		Feeling trapped
	Desire to isolate socially		Feelings of inadequacy
	Difficulty calming down after upset		Frequent feelings of impatience
	Difficulty focusing on task		Having racing thoughts
	Feeling burdened		Intolerant of interruptions
	Feeling frightened without reason		Often feeling on the verge of panic
	Feeling irritable, annoyed, or angry		Often worried about making a fool of self
	Feeling out of control		Tendency to overreact
	Feeling overwhelmed		

Please note that these mental and emotional symptoms may be signs of other types of mental or emotional illness. See your doctor to determine whether there is another cause for your symptoms.

If you have checked a lot of boxes in any of these three assessments, that may be a sign that your "check engine light" is on—giving you a warning that you are experiencing significant stress in your life that you need to examine and work at reducing.

This chapter provided some strategies for coping better with the stress in your life—stress that can contribute to excessive anger. Consider re-reading it when you're feeling stressed to remind yourself of the various techniques you can employ to cope with stress.

> *Anger is meant to alert us and not to damage us.*
> *It gives us detailed information about ourselves.*
>
> – MARIA L. VEGA

CHAPTER 4
Emotional Intelligence

Next, you will be following the directions on your roadmap that will help you become more emotionally intelligent—not only in the workplace, but in other areas of your life.

Emotional intelligence is defined as a set of competencies people possess (or learn) that help them recognize their behaviors, moods, and impulses, and best manage them according to the situation. Emotional intelligence is also the ability to understand the emotions of others and to navigate social situations.[23] Moment to moment, your thoughts have a tremendous impact on your level of emotional intelligence.

WHAT IS EMOTIONAL INTELLIGENCE?

1. Do you understand your own emotions? Yes / No
2. Are you able to control your emotions? Yes / No
3. Can you gauge how other people feel? Yes / No
4. Are you open to other people's feelings? Yes / No

People with high emotional intelligence can manage their own impulses, communicate with others effectively, manage change well, solve problems, and use humor to build rapport in tense situations. These people also have empathy and remain optimistic even in the face of adversity. At work, emotionally intelligent people are good at educating and persuading in a sales situation and at resolving customer complaints in a customer service role.

Emotional intelligence involves personal competence and social competence and is built upon four core skills: self-awareness, self-management, social awareness, and relationship management.[24]

Self-Awareness

Self-awareness increases your understanding of your strengths, weaknesses, and limitations. At work, self-aware leaders and managers practice mindfulness, respond rather than react, and try to shift their attention toward managing stress by regulating their thoughts, actions, tone of voice, level of stress, and communication.

Understanding your strengths as well as areas that need improvement can help you understand what motivates and satisfies you as well as help you understand what situations trigger your emotions.

What do you know about yourself? Identify five (each) of your strengths and weaknesses:

Strengths	Weaknesses
1.	1.
2.	2.
3.	3.
4.	4.
5.	5.

Studies have shown that your current ability to experience core feelings, such as anger, sadness, fear, and joy, often depends on the quality and consistency of your emotional experiences early in life. If your emotions were understood and valued at a young age, it is likely that your emotions have become valuable assets.

However, if your emotional experiences were confusing, threatening, or painful, you may have difficulty accessing and controlling those emotions today.[25]

To help you better understand how your earliest emotional experiences can affect you today, answer the following questions:

When you were young, were your emotions understood and valued?

_____

_____

_____

_____

Describe how your parents handled the emotion of anger:

_____

_____

_____

_____

When you were growing up, were you able to express your anger and speak about it?

_____

_____

_____

_____

Self-Management

Self-management is a skill that first requires self-awareness. The ability to stay flexible and direct your behavior in a positive way, even when you are experiencing difficult emotions, involves utilizing self-awareness skills and learning to control your emotions in healthy ways.

Such self-management also requires managing stress and learning how to understand your own anger.

When someone is overwhelmed by stress, it is more difficult for them to think clearly or to make rational decisions. Although our brains can handle feeling and thinking at the same time, stress can take us out of our comfort zone and into danger areas if not recognized.

> *Always include logic when dealing with emotions.*

Being able to understand and manage anger as well as other emotions is essential to maintaining relationships, and self-control is critical to successfully managing emotions such as anger, worry, anxiety, and frustration.

By understanding and practicing self-awareness, you will be able to receive disturbing pieces of information without letting it override your thoughts or undermine your self-control. You will also learn to make choices that allow you to control impulsive feelings and behaviors, manage your emotions in healthy ways, take initiative, follow through on commitments, and adapt to changing circumstances.

Describe an occasion when you mismanaged a situation:

_____

_____

_____

_____

For that situation, what might an emotionally intelligent response have looked like?

_____

_____

_____

_____

_____

Social Awareness

Being socially aware involves assessing situations and people, increasing active listening, focusing on body language, and connecting body language with words. Ask yourself: *Do my body language and my words tell the same story*?

It is also important to be able to empathize with those around you and try to understand why they feel the way they do. This involves the ability to understand what is really going on in the room and includes acknowledging the emotions of others, being thoughtful and respectful, and making decisions that take the feelings of others into consideration.

Studies have shown that that 55% of human communication is body language, 38% is tone of voice, and 7% are spoken words.[26] What we can learn from that is that being able to read another person's nonverbal cues is a key to being socially aware. Being aware of body language might even help you figure out what other people are thinking.

Socially aware people have empathy. According to Coaching Leaders Ltd., "Empathy is the ability to sense, understand, and respond to what other people are feeling."[27] But before someone can be empathetic, they must have self-awareness. If you can't read your own emotions, you won't be able to read the emotions of others.

Socially aware people also know how to listen patiently as the other person makes a point. Remaining objective and neutral while listening can also shine a light on your own beliefs and values. Listening to the opinions of other people—especially those you don't agree with—can help you learn about yourself.

Describe a situation when you were especially good at 1) reading someone's body language, 2) showed empathy, or 3) listened to a point of view you did not agree with, without interrupting with your own opinion. What was the outcome of that situation?

_____

_____

_____

_____

_____

Relationship Management

Awareness of your emotions and the emotions of others is essential to the development and maintenance of good relationships. Once emotional awareness is achieved, it becomes possible to maintain relationships that are more effective and fulfilling. Relationship management also requires the ability to behave cordially, even with people you don't like. This requires clear communication, the ability to inspire and influence others, and the ability to manage interactions successfully.

Relationship management sometimes also means leading others successfully, working at developing others, effective communication, learning how to manage conflict, and creating bonds.

People often think of relationship management in terms of working relationships, but developing effective relationship management skills can also help you with family, friends, and other personal relationships.

Improving relationships often means putting together, with relationship management, all the other aspects of emotional intelligence: self-awareness, self-management, and social awareness. That's why the awareness and understanding of nonverbal messages becomes valuable in improving relationships.

Furthermore, consider using humor and laughter to help manage yourself and your relationships. They are natural antidotes to stress and can be effective in bringing your nervous system into balance, reducing tension, calming you down, sharpening your mind, and making you more empathic. Humor can even reverse the effects of the fight-or-flight response.[28]

Describe a time when you mismanaged a relationship:

_____

_____

_____

_____

_____

Problematic Statements

Part of social awareness and relationship management is to avoid making problematic statements. These are phrases that contain words like *always* and *never* and *why*. Often, problematic statements can escalate and quickly become fighting words. Take a moment and think about how words might be restated and therefore become positive suggestions instead. Here are some examples:

- *Instead of* "You must . . ." *try saying* "Could we try this . . . ?"

- *Instead of* "You shouldn't . . ." *try putting the statement in the form of a question*: "What if we did this instead . . . ?"

- *Instead of* "You always (do this) . . ." *try saying* "I'm not handling what you're doing very well . . ."

Setting Goals for Your Relationships

Goal setting is an essential tool for self-motivation and self-management. It provides a roadmap for where you are going and how you plan to get there. Setting goals is linked to achieving success and is key to attaining the results you want.

Goals are easier to achieve when they are clear, specific, and broken down into steps you can manage and measure. It helps to start with an understanding of what you bring to a relationship, then make a list of goals for that relationship, and finally, to check your progress toward attaining those goals. Below, define specific steps toward your goals for one of your relationships:

Step No. 1: Understand yourself.

Examine one work or personal relationship. What are your strengths in that relationship?

_____

_____

_____

_____

What are your weaknesses in the relationship?

_____

_____

_____

_____

Step No. 2: Make clear, specific goals for your current (work or personal) relationships.

Describe your relationship goals:

_____

_____

_____

_____

Step No. 3: Check your progress.

Evaluate your progress toward your goals. Are you doing what needs to be done to meet them? If not, what can you do to get back on target? Incorporate the ideas of self-awareness and self-management.

_____

_____

_____

_____

Check your emotional intelligence quotient (EQ) on the next page.

EXERCISE – CHAPTER 4

CHECK YOUR EMOTIONAL INTELLIGENCE

Instructions: *This exercise is intended as another way to monitor your "check engine light." It will help you understand your level of emotional intelligence (EQ) and assist you in determining both your strengths and where you can put additional effort toward improvement. Put a checkmark next to those statements that are mostly true of you. If a statement is not generally true of you, place an X in the blank space next to it.*

No one else will see this exercise, unless you decide to share it, so be as honest in your self-assessment as possible.

SELF-AWARENESS

___ Life generally makes sense to me.

___ I can easily articulate what I am feeling.

___ I understand my motivations and feelings, so I can easily explain my actions.

___ I see myself similarly to the way others see me.

___ I often agree with or can easily accept the feedback I receive from others.

SELF-MANAGEMENT

___ I am generally content in life.

___ I almost always stay calm even when circumstances become difficult.

___ It takes a lot to irritate me.

___ I rarely feel rage or strike out at others (verbally or physically).

___ I rarely feel myself spinning out of control or regret my actions.

SOCIAL AWARENESS

___ Even when we don't always see eye-to-eye, people generally respect and like me.

___ I can keep calm and respond appropriately when other people are emotional.

___ It's not difficult for me to talk to people I don't know well.

___ I feel comfortable leading a meeting or speaking in front of a group when necessary.

___ I can be persuasive when necessary—without being manipulative.

EMPATHY

    ___ I have several friends and family members whom I can ask for help when necessary.

    ___ I am able to mirror the feelings of others; in other words, I can experience and show empathy to them.

    ___ Based on body language, I can usually tell how someone else is feeling.

    ___ Based on their body language, most of the time I am correct about how other people see me.

    ___ I pay close attention and listen well to another person during a conversation.

RELATIONSHIP MANAGEMENT

    ___ I feel comfortable talking to almost everyone.

    ___ When someone becomes emotional, I can easily take it in stride.

    ___ I rarely come across a difficult person.

    ___ I rarely lose my cool when I encounter an incompetent person.

    ___ I am always looking for a way to make sure each situation works well for all sides.

SETTING GOALS

    ___ It is important to me to have time to myself to think every day.

    ___ I feel good about the way my career is going.

    ___ I have clearly defined objectives for my future.

    ___ I work every day toward achieving my objectives.

    ___ Every day I look forward to someday reaching my goals.

Instructions: *Use the lists on the two previous pages to fill out the chart below. For each category, enter each check mark under "Areas of Strength" and each "X" under "Areas for Improvement."*

Once you have filled in all your check marks and Xs, take note of where you see more check marks and where you see more Xs. Your areas of strength are where you see more check marks. Anything marked with an X can be considered an area for improvement.

Use this information to make decisions about where to concentrate your efforts in improving your EQ. Your goal is to have zero Xs.

SUBJECT AREA	"√" AREAS OF STRENGTH	"X" AREAS FOR IMPROVEMENT
Self-Awareness		
Self-Management		
Social Awareness		
Empathy		
Relationship Management		
Setting Goals		

Write down your areas of strength:

1. _____
2. _____
3. _____
4. _____
5. _____
6. _____

Write down your areas for improvement:

1. _____
2. _____
3. _____
4. _____
5. _____
6. _____

> *How we express anger and respond to it is a result of the behaviors we have learned.*
> – MARIA L. VEGA

CHAPTER 5

Nonverbal vs. Verbal Communication

The next step on the roadmap is understanding that good communication is the foundation of any successful relationship, be it personal or professional. It is the process by which people verbally or nonverbally share information and ideas. Others can tell whether you care, if you're telling the truth, and even how well you're listening by the way you move your body, the way you look, and how you react to them.

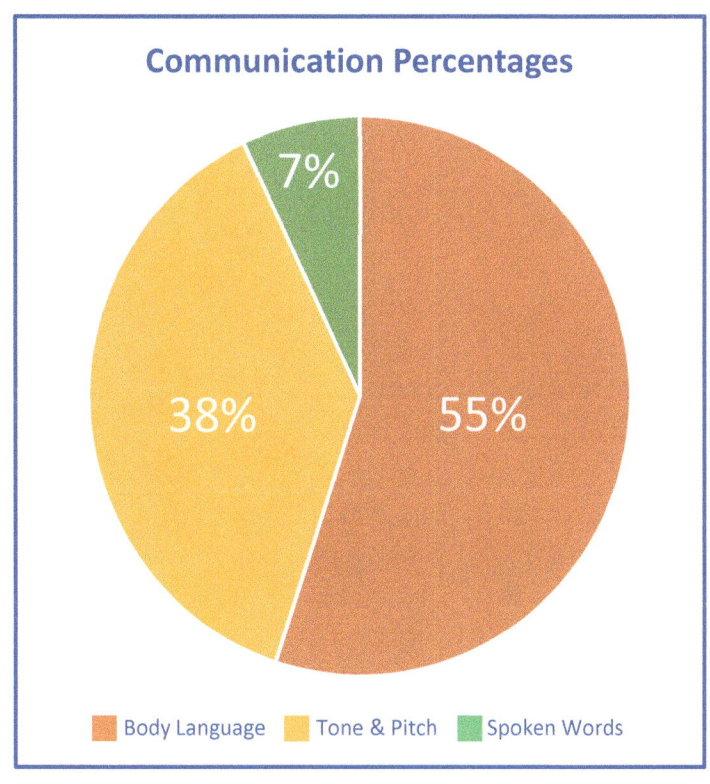

Nonverbal Communication

When your nonverbal signals match up with the words you are saying, they increase trust, clarity, and rapport. To become a better communicator, learn to read the body language and nonverbal cues of others and be aware of your own nonverbal signals.

A study by Dr. Albert Mehrabian and colleague Susan Ferris determined that communication on average is based on **55% body language, 38% tone and pitch**, and **7% spoken words**.[29]

How Do We Communicate?

We communicate in three major ways:

- **Verbal:** This is what you are saying, i.e., your words, **7%**.

- **Paraverbal:** What you say is the verbal portion. *How* you say it—your tone, speed, pitch, and volume—is the paraverbal portion, **38%**.

- **Nonverbal:** The gestures and body language that accompany your words are also a type of communication, though it is nonverbal. Some examples include hunched shoulders, folded arms, or repeated foot-tapping, **55%**.

Paraverbal Communication

The Global Training Institute provides an exercise for understanding paraverbal communication: Have you ever heard the saying, "It's not what you say, it's how you say it"? Try saying these three sentences out loud, placing the emphasis on the underlined word.

- "**I** didn't say you were wrong." (Implying it wasn't me.)

- "I didn't **say** you were wrong." (Implying I communicated it in another way.)

- "I didn't say you were **wrong**." (Implying I said something else.)[30]

Nonverbal Communication

Nonverbal communication is a natural, unconscious part of language that can often express true feelings and intentions. The ability to understand and use nonverbal communication, or body language, is a powerful tool that can help you connect with others, express what you really mean, and build better relationships. Nonverbal communication can be best described as a silent form of communicating without using any form of speech.

Facial expressions, gestures, eye contact, posture, and tone of voice are all forms of nonverbal communication. These nonverbal cues can complement, regulate, substitute for, or accent a verbal message. Often, it is someone's nonverbal communication that speaks the loudest.

Nonverbal communication can act as a substitute for a verbal message. Nonverbal messages can also contradict a verbal message.[31] What comes out of your mouth and what you communicate through your body language can sometimes be completely different. When faced with such mixed signals, the listener must choose whether to believe one message over the other: verbal or nonverbal.

Facial Expressions

Facial expressions and eye contact are especially effective when communicating nonverbally. Without saying a word, facial expressions, which are universal across cultures, can communicate a range of feelings, including:

Affection	Anger	Anxiety	Attraction
Disgust	Fear	Happiness	Hostility
Interest	Sadness	Surprise	Worry

Additional examples include:

- Smiles and frowns often speak as well as or better than words.

- A raised eyebrow can mean inquisitiveness, curiosity, or disbelief.

- Chewing one's lips can indicate thinking, or it can be a sign of boredom, anxiety, or nervousness.

List some things you can tell from a person's facial expression:

___
___
___
___
___
___

Body Language

Body language is an extremely broad term that simply means the way in which our body speaks to others. Yet it is 55% of how we communicate.

Our perceptions of people are influenced by the way they sit, walk, stand, or hold their head, all of which communicate a wealth of information. Body language can include arm position, stance, posture, and other subtle movements that can express aggressive, assertive, or passive attitudes. Is a person's body relaxed or stiff? Are his/her shoulders tense and raised or relaxed?

Because body language can make someone feel comfortable or threatened, it is important to be conscious of how your body "speaks" to others. Using the right body language can also be an important part of conflict resolution.

A good goal is to present yourself in a way that makes other people feel comfortable, safe, and willing to engage as partners in the process, especially when attempting to resolve a conflict.

Standing or Sitting

Think for a moment about different body postures and the messages they relay.

What do the following examples of body language mean?

- Sitting hunched over. This may indicate stress or discomfort.

- Leaning back when standing or sitting. This may indicate a casual and relaxed demeanor.

- Standing straight with shoulders back. This usually means someone is confident.[32]

Position of Arms, Legs, Feet, and Hands

When people do the following, what does it mean to you?

- Cross their arms.

- Fidget.

- Run a hand through their hair.

Touch and Personal Space

When there is physical contact between people, it is important to know if it is appropriate to the situation. A weak handshake, a warm hug, a reassuring touch on the back, and a patronizing pat on the head all communicate something different.

In the same way, invading a person's space by standing too close can make him or her feel uncomfortable or communicate affection or dominance. Acceptance of this type of nonverbal communication varies with culture.[33]

Describe your culture's expectations for touch and personal space:

_____

_____

_____

_____

Eye Contact

Eyes may express affection, hostility, or interest, which means that making eye contact with another person is especially important during a conversation. Eye contact is also important for maintaining the flow of conversation. Be aware of your eye contact with others. Is it overly intense, or does it seem normal? What is your culture's expectation for eye contact?

Gestures and Posture

A gesture is a nonverbal message that is made with a specific part of the body. Waving and pointing are examples of how we use our hands to communicate. Hand gestures can also be used to express anger or be dismissive.

As discussed earlier, though facial expressions tend to be similar across cultures, gestures differ greatly from region to region and from culture to culture. This can be important to know when you're traveling, whether for pleasure or business.

According to *Business Insider*, "Sometimes, making what you think is an innocent gesture in one country can land you in hot water somewhere else. Just ask any traveler who's given a thumbs-up in Afghanistan. Or someone who's crossed their fingers in Vietnam or signaled 'OK' in Brazil. All those gestures have offensive connotations away from American soil."[34]

Voice

Another form of nonverbal communication involves the voice. Does the person's voice project warmth, confidence, and interest, or is it strained? Does the person's voice seem flat, cool, and disinterested? Are his/her intonations over-the-top dramatic? Without words, it is possible to add sarcasm, disapproval, and even laughter that will affect someone's engagement in a conversation.

Emotional Awareness

To send accurate nonverbal cues, it helps to be aware of your emotions and to be able to recognize the emotions of others and the true signals they are sending. Emotional awareness assists in creating trust in relationships by helping you to send nonverbal signals that match up with your words. These nonverbal messages can also show others that you understand and care or indicate to others that the relationship is meeting your emotional needs.

Learning to read nonverbal signals and body language may help identify inconsistencies in communication. For instance, is someone saying one thing verbally while his/her body language is saying something else?

In addition to paying attention to nonverbal signals, it is also advisable to trust your instincts. If you get the sense that someone isn't being honest or that something seems off, you may be picking up on a mismatch between verbal and nonverbal signals. Note the image below. Is there a mismatch in the communication of either of the people in the photograph?

Using "I" Messages

How you frame your messages can greatly increase your ability to communicate. How would you react to the following statements?

- You should rethink that outfit.

- You speak too softly; nobody can understand you.

- You should work at being more organized.

It's easy to understand why many people would feel hurt and react negatively to such statements; after all, they put all the blame on the other person. These statements can also make the speaker seem arrogant and superior.

Instead of starting a sentence with "you," try using an "I message." This format places the responsibility with the speaker, makes a clear statement, and offers constructive feedback.

Here is an example: Instead of saying, "Please speak up, I can't hear you," say, "I often have difficulty hearing you when you speak at a low volume."

Be careful not to start your sentence with some form of: "You, who, what, when, why, never, or always . . . ." Those kinds of statements tend to create feelings of blame and a sense of injustice in the receiver.

Check your interpretation of body language on the next page.

EXERCISE – CHAPTER 5

INTERPRETING BODY LANGUAGE

Instructions: In the "Interpretation" column below, describe what each listed gesture means to you.

GESTURE	INTERPRETATION
Nodding head	
Shaking head	
Moving head from side to side	
Shrugging shoulders	
Crossed arms	
Tapping hands or fingers	
Thumbs up	
Thumbs down	
Pointing middle finger (vertically)	
Handshake	
Flap of the hand	
Waving hand	
Waving both hands over head	
Crossed legs or ankles	
Tapping toes or feet	

> *Bad communication can destroy a good relationship.*
>
> – MARIA L. VEGA

CHAPTER 6
Developing Effective Communication

A roadmap is full of all kinds of communication: place names, distances between towns, and notable places to visit. That kind of communication is relatively simple, but communication between people is far more complex. Yet communicating well is a vital skill—one everyone should master—considering that effective communication can:

- Improve productivity.

- Increase your ability to solve problems.

- Decrease your level of stress.

- Improve your relationships with others.

- Increase your level of satisfaction with life.

- Improve your ability to meet goals and achieve dreams.

Overcoming Common Barriers to Good Communication

A good place to start is to learn how to overcome common barriers to effective communication, which can include differences in language, culture, and location.

<u>Language</u> – Language differences can become a barrier to communication not only when the people communicating speak different languages but frequently

when people are communicating in a language not native to them. Even when people speak the same language, if they are from different regions and speak in different dialects with unique subtleties of speech and idioms, they also may find that communication suddenly becomes complicated.

Identify a few strategies that could minimize the language barrier (for example, using pictures or graphs or hiring a translator):

_____

_____

_____

_____

Culture – There can also be times when people speak the same language but are from different cultures in which words or gestures can have different meanings. Or the people might be of a different socioeconomic status or have vastly different lifestyles. All these things can hinder the ability to get across a message effectively. If you are able to prepare ahead of the time when you will be communicating with someone new, find out as much as you can about the other person's culture and background and how it differs from yours.

List some possible areas of misunderstanding when communicating between cultures and how to prevent or resolve those problems:

_____

_____

_____

_____

The Foundation of Effective Communication: Active Listening

In today's high-speed, high-tech, high-stress world, communicating well is more important than ever. Many people consider speaking to be the most important element of communication. However, good listening skills are critical; being a good listener not only helps you better understand what other people are trying to convey, it also improves your rapport with others and can even strengthen your problem-solving skills.

Active listening helps build relationships, solve problems, ensures understanding, improves accuracy, and can resolve conflicts. Parents who practice active listening can help their children become resourceful, self-reliant adults who can solve their own problems.

Listening also builds friendships and careers. It saves marriages and even helps save money.

Active listening involves hearing and paying attention to the speaker. However, hearing what someone says and effective listening are quite different abilities. Active listening begins with paying attention.

Become a more successful listener by clearing your mind, focusing on what the other person is saying, not interrupting, and using appropriate body language by

keeping good eye contact, leaning forward, and avoiding distracting behaviors such as playing with a pencil or drumming your fingers.

Here are some additional tips that will make you a more successful active listener:

- Pay attention to the speaker's nonverbal messages.

- Respond but don't react.

- Respond constructively.

- Encourage the other person to speak by asking questions.

- Paraphrase what you think the other person has said.

The following are some tips that will make you a more successful communicator overall:

- Be positive and open. Share your feelings truthfully but respectfully.

- Quickly acknowledge responses from the other person.

- Respond constructively and appropriately. Don't simply "react."

- Be organized in what you are communicating.

- Avoid jargon, colloquialisms, and overcomplicated terminology.

- Encourage open-ended conversation. Ask questions that require more than a one-word answer.

Communicating Assertively

How does someone recognize assertive communication? It is a learned skill that is built on mutual respect. It happens when people state their opinions and feelings clearly and affirm their own needs without harming others or stepping all over someone else's rights.

Assertiveness allows you to express ideas and feelings in an open, honest, and direct way. Individuals who practice assertive communication value themselves and their time and are strong advocates for themselves while at the same time being respectful of the rights of others. Learning to communicate assertively can build your self-esteem.

Communicating assertively means conveying your message clearly and calmly without being too passive or too aggressive. Assertiveness does not guarantee you will receive what you want, but it does make it more likely. The idea is to be clear and direct, to describe how the other person's actions make you feel, and to keep pressing for what you want. Here are some pointers:

- Recognize that your needs matter too.

- Speak up and ask for what you want, but also be willing to listen.

- Stand up for yourself.

- Express your point clearly and confidently.

- Make sure the result is fair for you as well as for others, yet realize you may have to compromise.

Being assertive enables you to do all of the following amazing things:

- Act in your own best interest.

- Clearly express your rights.

- Demonstrate self-respect by exercising your rights.

- Expect respect from others.

- Consider the needs and rights of others.

- Include the right to refuse a request.

- Develop and expect trust.

- Negotiate a mutually acceptable compromise.

To practice effective, assertive communication, face the person you are speaking with and maintain eye contact. Be present and attentive, and mentally screen out distractions. Additional suggestions for effective communication include:

- Use confident, positive body language.

- Verbalize a clear, confident message.

- Learn to say no when appropriate.

- Use a firm, pleasant, clear, and appropriately audible tone of voice.

- State the issue and the outcome you would like to achieve.

- Stay focused.

- Validate the other person's feelings and issues.

- Summarize or restate the other person's point of view.

- When speaking, make certain that you have the other person's attention.

- Be organized and prepared.

- Use "I" phrases such as "I need . . ." and "I feel . . . ."

- Encourage open-ended conversation by avoiding yes-no questions.

- Share your feelings truthfully.

- Be specific and identify the issue at hand.

- Be positive.

- Respond rather than simply react.

- Ask for a summary of the points the other person is making.

- Try to resolve conflicts rather than win them.

Assertive Communication

Assertive communication is a learned skill. The more you practice it, the better you will become. Assertive behavior is built on mutual respect and demonstrates that you are sensitive to the rights of others and willing to work constructively together. The results are worth it: trust, acceptance, and cooperation.

Check the next page to see if you have an assertive communication style.

EXERCISE – CHAPTER 6

ASSERTIVE STYLES

Assertive people are confident, clear, and in control of themselves. They address problems directly and seek fair resolutions. They know their rights and respect the rights of other people. Their needs are usually met without hurting other people.

Instructions: *Below is a list of behaviors and characteristics that are common among people with assertive styles of dealing with conflict. Think about each characteristic and check whether it sounds like you* most of the time, sometimes, *or* rarely.

This is true of me:

	Most of the time	Sometimes	Rarely
1. I pay careful attention to my feelings and express them directly and honestly.			
2. People usually know where they stand with me but do not feel judged by me.			
3. I feel in control of my emotions.			
4. I stand up for my rights while respecting the rights of others.			
5. When in a conflict, I tend to use "I" messages rather than blaming "you" statements.			
6. I usually have a clear idea of what I want.			
7. I make good eye contact when speaking with others.			
8. I have good posture.			
9. I can listen to and consider another person's point of view without interrupting.			
10. I can say "no" without feeling guilty.			
11. I try to obtain all the facts before jumping to conclusions or making decisions.			
12. My intimate relationships tend to be based on equal partnerships.			
13. When I have something to complain about, I try to offer a solution as well.			
14. When I criticize someone, I try to constructively focus on the behavior, not the person.			
15. I maintain my personal space boundaries and respect others' boundaries.			
16. I am generally confident about myself.			
17. I speak in a clear, even-toned voice.			
18. I may not always get what I want, but most often my needs are met.			
19. I can respond to criticism without getting angry or defensive.			
20. I can apologize when I know I'm wrong.			

Give yourself two (2) points for each statement that applies to you **most of the time**, *one (1) point for every* **sometimes** *answer, and zero (0) points for every* **rarely** *answer.*

YOUR SCORE: _____

© 2003 Wellness Reproductions and Publishing. Used by permission.

Passive Communication

Passive communication is a style in which individuals have developed a pattern of avoidance of expressing opinions or feelings, protecting their rights, and identifying and meeting their needs. As a result, passive individuals do not respond overtly to hurtful or anger-inducing situations. This allows grievances and annoyances to mount and could lead to an explosive outburst, which may be out of proportion to the triggering incident. After the outburst, they may feel shame, guilt, and confusion, so they return to being passive.

Check the next page to see if you have a passive communication style.

EXERCISE – CHAPTER 6

PASSIVE STYLES

Passive people are generally indirect, anxious, and inhibited. They often do not address problems with others and do not speak up for their own rights. Other people often respond to this behavior by taking advantage of or ignoring the passive person. Sometimes passive people's anger will build up inside, and they will eventually explode or develop problems such as depression, physical aches and pains, or anxiety.

Instructions: *Below is a list of behaviors and characteristics that are common among people with passive styles of dealing with conflict. Think about each characteristic and check whether it sounds like you* most of the time, sometimes, *or* rarely.

This is true of me:

	Most of the time	Sometimes	Rarely
1. I have a hard time saying no to people.			
2. I often say "nothing's wrong" when it is.			
3. I don't usually let others know my problems.			
4. I often assume I'm wrong when there's a conflict with someone else.			
5. I often look at the ground when someone I'm upset with or intimidated by is talking to me.			
6. I often find myself being interrupted or "talked over."			
7. I feel paralyzed when directly confronted with a conflict.			
8. I tend to have poor posture (slouching or slumping).			
9. I withhold information from people I'm upset with.			
10. I often question whether my opinions are valid.			
11. I often feel resentful of other people.			
12. I will walk out rather than deal with conflict.			
13. I sometimes apologize even if I don't believe I'm wrong.			
14. I try to avoid conversation about sensitive or controversial topics.			
15. I suffer from frequent headaches or stomach aches.			
16. When I'm upset with someone close to me, they usually don't even know it.			
17. I often have a hard time sleeping.			
18. I tend to feel depressed.			
19. I have a hard time speaking up for my rights.			
20. Other people often take advantage of me.			

Give yourself two (2) points for each statement that applies to you **most of the time***, one (1) point for every* **sometimes** *answer, and zero (0) points for every* **rarely** *answer.*

YOUR SCORE: _____

© 2003 Wellness Reproductions and Publishing. Used by permission.

Aggressive Communication

Aggressive communication is a style in which individuals express their feelings and opinions and advocate for their needs in a way that violates the rights of others. Thus, aggressive communicators are verbally and/or physically abusive. Such individuals may try to dominate others; can be impulsive; may speak in a loud, demanding, and overbearing voice; and might interrupt frequently or not listen well.

Check the next page to see if you have an aggressive communication style.

EXERCISE – CHAPTER 6

AGGRESSIVE STYLES

Aggressive people are sometimes threatening and antagonistic toward others. They are often bossy and dominating, loud, sarcastic, and frequently blame others rather than accepting responsibility for their part in a conflict. Other people react to aggressive people by feeling hurt, humiliated, or threatened and sometimes respond with anger or vengeance. Often, aggressive people do not gain the respect of others. While they may seem to get their way, in the long run, they do not have the support of others.

Instructions: *Below is a list of behaviors and characteristics that are common among people with aggressive styles of dealing with conflict. Think about each characteristic and check whether it sounds like* you *most of the time,* sometimes, *or* rarely.

This is true of me:

#	Statement	Most of the time	Sometimes	Rarely
1.	I tend to speak loudly, especially when I'm trying to get a point across.			
2.	I'm known to be opinionated and blunt.			
3.	I have a hard time keeping my opinion to myself.			
4.	When I want something, I go after it no matter what.			
5.	I have a history of getting into physical fights.			
6.	When in conflict, I tend to physically move toward the other person.			
7.	I tend to have an "I don't care" attitude about other people's feelings.			
8.	I tend to interrupt other people.			
9.	I can be very sarcastic.			
10.	I tend to be bossy.			
11.	When in a confrontation, my eye contact could be said to be glaring.			
12.	I often use "you" messages, telling other people what they are thinking or doing wrong.			
13.	I rarely admit I'm wrong or apologize.			
14.	Other people tend to act vengeful toward me.			
15.	Sometimes I feel my anger is out of control.			
16.	I feel the need to be in control in my relationships.			
17.	I tend to give other people advice, whether they have asked for it.			
18.	Sometimes I blame others for my problems			
19.	When someone criticizes me, my natural reaction is to defend myself by criticizing back.			
20.	When I think someone is wrong, I can't wait to tell them about it.			

Give yourself two (2) points for each statement that applies to you **most of the time**, *one (1) point for every* **sometimes** *answer, and zero (0) points for every* **rarely** *answer.*

YOUR SCORE: _____

© 2003 Wellness Reproductions and Publishing. Used by permission.

Passive-Aggressive Communication

Passive-aggressive communication is a style in which individuals appear passive on the surface but are really acting out anger in a subtle, indirect, or behind-the-scenes way. People who develop a pattern of passive-aggressive communication usually feel powerless, stuck, and resentful. They may feel incapable of dealing directly with the object of their resentments and instead express their anger in a subtle way.

Sometimes a person's passive-aggressive communication comes out in the form of sarcastic or negative humor or even as gaslighting, which is, according to *Psychology Today*, "a form of persistent manipulation and brainwashing that causes the victim to doubt her or himself, and ultimately their sense of perception, identity, and self-worth."[35]

Check the next page to see if you have a passive-aggressive communication style.

EXERCISE – CHAPTER 6

PASSIVE-AGGRESSIVE STYLES

Passive-aggressive people do not address problems directly but try to "get back at" the person they are upset with in a way that will hurt the other person without drawing attention to themselves. Because these people do not address the real problem, their needs are rarely met.

Instructions: *Below is a list of behaviors and characteristics that are common among people with passive-aggressive styles of dealing with conflict. Think about each characteristic and check whether it sounds like you most of the time, sometimes, or rarely.*

This is true of me:

		Most of the time	Sometimes	Rarely
1.	I often sulk and pout.			
2.	I tend to talk about people behind their backs.			
3.	I often give people the "silent treatment" when I'm upset with them.			
4.	In an intimate relationship, I might punish my partner by withholding affection.			
5.	I procrastinate a lot.			
6.	I usually pretend everything's okay even when it's not.			
7.	If I'm angry with someone close to me, they will know it, but they may not know why.			
8.	When I'm angry with someone, I will just stop talking to them.			
9.	I believe in the phrase "Don't get mad, get even."			
10.	I don't like to draw attention to myself when I'm upset.			
11.	I tend to be suspicious and distrustful of others.			
12.	I tend to let my anger fester until I plan to get back at the other person.			
13.	When I'm upset with someone, I refuse to make eye contact with them.			
14.	When I'm upset with someone, I purposely do little things that I know are annoying.			
15.	I can really hold a grudge.			
16.	If I see someone I'm upset with, I might turn and go in the other direction to avoid them.			
17.	I'm not good at expressing my feelings.			
18.	I sometimes get involved with behind-the-scenes troublemaking.			
19.	I do clever things to get back at people.			
20.	When I'm upset with someone, I might say yes to them but not do what I agreed to.			

*Give yourself two (2) points for each statement that applies to you **most of the time**, one (1) point for every **sometimes** answer, and zero (0) points for every **rarely** answer.*

YOUR SCORE: _____

© 2003 Wellness Reproductions and Publishing. Used by permission.

What is Your Style of Communication?

To improve your self-awareness, describe the style of communication you most often use and the impact it has in your relationships:

_____

_____

_____

_____

_____

_____

> *My goal is to create a culture of happy individuals who in turn bring positive energy into their relationships, their jobs, and their lives.*
>
> – MARIA L. VEGA

CHAPTER 7
Managing Relationships

When you think about managing your relationships, do you first think about *control* or about *emotional intelligence*? The truth is that the only person we have any real control over is ourselves—in that case, why do we even talk about *managing* our relationships? Of course, what we're really discussing is managing our own actions related to our relationships.

To do so effectively means employing an understanding of all of what we have already studied in this workbook—the causes of anger, triggers, stress, communication, and emotional intelligence—in order to work at creating more satisfying relationships. It will also take all the other aspects of emotional intelligence—self-awareness, self-management, social awareness, and empathy—in order to manage your relationships successfully.

But is it worth it? How well you manage your relationships directly correlates with how well you manage stress and anger and your ability to listen and empathize with your spouse, partner, family members, and coworkers.

While it's true that difficult people can be found in almost any situation, dealing with our closest associates can be particularly challenging. Those are the relationships that are often the most stressful. What follows are suggestions for building and maintaining stronger relationships with those you care about most. That, in turn, will help you as you seek to manage your strongest emotions.

Develop a Positive Attitude

Let's begin with us, since we are the only ones we can control. Part of self-management is working toward improving our own attitudes. It isn't always easy to keep a positive mental outlook, especially in the face of difficulty. In fact, studies have indicated that we are naturally hardwired to focus on the negative, which means it often takes focus to overcome that tendency.[36]

For example, when a reckless driver cuts you off, your feeling of anger may stay with you for a while. But there are strategic actions you can take to change your focus. Instead of dwelling on the negative, take note of small gestures of kindness. For instance, when someone greets you with a smile or holds the door open for you, make a conscious note of it and allow a feeling of appreciation to take over, even if the gesture is small.

Additionally, cultivating an "attitude of gratitude" can improve your sense of well-being and shift your state of mind toward positivity. To practice this, write in a gratitude journal. Each day, list three to five things for which you are grateful. Developing this discipline can increase your peace of mind and deflect negative ideas that may creep into your thoughts, which in turn affect your feelings. As an incentive to help you maintain the journal, choose a small reward to give yourself after you have maintained the journal for a week.

Let's start right here. List three things that you're currently grateful for:

1. _____

2. _____

3. _____

Additionally, take a moment each day to note what's going right in your life. Doing this daily will help you make it a habit that could change your life for the better. Did you know the average amount of time to make a habit automatic is around two months? However, if you miss a day, simply take note of why you missed it and keep working at establishing this good habit.

Describe one thing that is going well for you right now (finances, career, relationship, friendships, physically, etc.):

_____

_____

_____

_____

Practicing both of these strategies—journaling your gratitude and describing what is going well in your life—will inevitably have a positive impact on your attitude and, in turn, your relationships.

Handling Someone Else's Negativity

In all relationships, you will encounter times when another person communicates with you in a way that you perceive as negative. They may express a difficult emotion, make a sarcastic or hurtful comment, or raise their voice or shout.

In *Emotional Intelligence 2.0*, Travis Bradberry and Jean Greaves write, "One key to managing relationships is leaning into your own discomfort and taking a moment to acknowledge, not stifle or change, other people's feelings . . . acknowledge emotions without making them a big deal, marginalizing them, or dismissing them. Everyone has a right to experience feelings, even if you might not feel the same way. You don't have to agree with the way people are feeling, but you do have to recognize those feelings as legitimate and respect them."[37]

STRATEGIES FOR RESPONDING WITH EMOTIONAL INTELLIGENCE

- Think before you respond.
- Calmly and clearly explain why you feel the way you do or what you think the problem is.
- Don't yell, use insults, or make threats.
- Use "I" statements to tell the person how you feel, which avoids placing blame on someone else.
- Don't reinforce negativity by responding with negative words.
- Bear in mind that your choice of words can set the tone for the remainder of the conversation.
- Choose your words carefully. Instead of using a word like "frustrating," use a more positive alternative, such as "challenging," which communicates that the problem may be solvable.
- Don't hold a grudge after the disagreement. Be willing to forgive.
- Try to find a solution—together.

Active Listening and Empathy

The value of listening is often underestimated. However, listening involves more than simply hearing someone's words. In your personal relationships, develop active listening skills to ensure that you can hear your partner's, family member's, or coworker's words. Aspects of active listening were discussed in Chapter 6.

As a reminder to yourself, list some of the strategies for active listening here:

_____

_____

_____

_____

_____

Now that you are more aware of what will work better when anger arises, you can respond differently in how you express your emotions.

It would be ideal if you and your partner would take turns being angry, but we all know that's not realistic; in most relationships, when one person gets angry, the other one does too. That means that you may be the one who has to change things up.

A Suggestion for Action:

Therapist Irene Hansen Savarese suggests, "Your part is to be supportive, listen actively, and ask clarifying questions. Remind yourself that your partner is coming from his or her perspective and personal experiences . . . . If you are able to do this for your partner, I can assure you that you will see big, positive changes in your relationship. Perhaps your partner will initially react with surprise and even anger that you are changing your steps of the dance you have danced together for so many years of fighting. However, if you keep up your end of the relationship and focus on being the best partner you can be, your partner will eventually follow and give you the same courtesy when you are upset and need support."[38]

How to Respond to Withdrawal

It isn't just your partner who may employ what is commonly known as "the silent treatment." When you're upset, you may also get the impulse to hop in your car and drive away. Doing so removes you from the immediate conflict and may help you to calm down, but it is not beneficial for your relationship.

An alternative is to let your partner know that you're not avoiding talking to him or her but that it would be better for you to take a few minutes to calm down before you come back and continue the conversation. Just communicating that fact will help to ease any anxiety your partner may feel about your leaving.

But what can you do when it is the other person who slams the door and walks away? You may have to be patient. This is where practicing emotional intelligence pays off.

Dr. Kathleen Smith, a licensed professional counselor, writes, "If your partner tends to give you the silent treatment . . . you've probably experienced some anxiety not knowing what's going to happen. You can't make them talk to you, but

you can share that you're ready to share your thinking and work together when they're ready."[39]

Explain Your Decisions

Part of managing relationships often is as simple as remembering to communicate your intentions. This is true for both personal and professional relationships. At work you would like to create buy-in for your team's project. At home, you would like your partner to be supportive of a decision you would like to make. But in order for that to happen, people—especially adults—need to know why you have chosen to do something.

When you remain silent instead and take an action that will affect others, people often feel disrespected and believe that you don't trust them. This may be a difficult habit to break if you are used to making quick decisions and making them alone, which is actually a positive sign that you are capable and competent.

However, it can come across differently if someone is left without information.

At work, when changes are made that are likely to affect many people, employees are much more likely to feel a sense of connection and loyalty to an organization, or at least to their supervisor, when the proposed change is communicated openly and honestly ahead of time, even when a corporate decision will affect them negatively.

Emotional intelligence specialists Bradberry and Greaves write, "Instead of making a change and expecting others to just accept it, take time to explain the why behind the decision, including alternatives, and why the final choice made the most sense. If you can ask for ideas and input ahead of time, it's even better. Finally, acknowledge how the decision will affect everyone."[40] Try the following exercise to get you started at more effectively communicating your upcoming decisions.

<u>Instructions</u>: *This exercise requires you to identify any upcoming decisions that will need to be made in the next two to four months affecting others around you. It works for your job, for personal decision-making, or both. Next, determine which people at work or home will be affected by those decisions and add them to the list below. Then determine when you will speak to each and place a checkmark next to the name when your task is complete. When you communicate, be sure to include the reasons why the decision needs to be made, who will make it, and how and when it is likely to be carried out. If you can give people a chance to give their input, even better. Once each decision is made, be sure to communicate that as well.*

Date	Upcoming Decision	Who Needs to Be Told	When I Will Communicate	Done ✓

Continue to Be Aware of What Makes You Angry

Relationships are negatively affected by mismanaged anger. If you want to maintain better relationships, it can only help to grow in your awareness of what causes your anger, how you respond when you become angry, and how you react when someone else is angry with you. We have already discussed these aspects of anger in earlier chapters, but now it is important to recognize how such awareness will also help you to have and maintain better relationships.

The first thing to remember is that you have to understand your anger and recognize that when you are angry, it says something about *you* rather than what you are angry about. Once you accept that fact, you can then begin to recognize where your anger came from.

In the midst of an argument it is tempting to blame the person with whom you are angry. Your partner may very well be wrong, but the point is to focus on yourself. If you are willing to sweep your side of the street, so to speak, you are more likely to seek constructive solutions that allow you to work with rather than against your partner. **It may help to write down your angry thoughts and what led to them.**

Don't forget (see Chapter 1) that *anger is a secondary emotion*. Did your anger start with fear, sadness, hurt, rejection, or your own vulnerability? Anger often works as a defense against your primary emotion, especially when you feel vulnerable.

Many of us were raised to ignore our vulnerabilities. Letting yourself express uncontrolled anger is often the easy way out in the short run, but in the long term? It can negatively impact your relationships.[41]

One of the ways to think about anger in relationships is how your response affects others. If you want to be a good employer, employee, partner, or friend—it matters how you react when you're angry. Do you withdraw? Complain to a third person? Lash out verbally? Try to control the other person? Or do you decide in advance to take a more emotionally intelligent approach?

There are alternative, thoughtful actions you can take that will be much more effective in managing your anger and your response to anger in someone else, with the result that you are much more likely to experience happier, more successful relationships.

- First, instead of trying to calm the other person down when an argument heats up, **start with yourself**. Think about how you might react if someone tells you to "calm down" when you're angry—does it make you even more reactive?

  Instead, focus on managing your own reactions. Try some deep breathing. Let your partner know you need to calm down by taking a walk but that you'll return shortly when you're calmer.

- Second, Dr. Kathleen Smith argues, ". . . if you're angry with your partner and want them to change a behavior, your attempt at controlling them is likely to produce a negative reaction. The goal is to **share your thinking** with the hope that you'll be heard, not to shame the other person. Remember, it's unlikely that you will be heard if your words and behaviors are lighting up the fear-response in your partner's brain."[42]

- Finally, it is important to take as long as necessary to work out your conflict with your partner. **Take your time**. Hear what the other person has to say. Seek not to be right, but rather to connect. Focus on responding and not reacting by using emotional intelligence.

At the same time that you are seeking to act maturely and not let your anger control your responses, neither do you have to endure actual abuse or a tantrum from your partner, and you may even want to examine the value of the relationship.

Dr. Smith adds, "Maturity simply looks like being willing to not let your emotions totally run the show. It looks like asking, 'What is the best version of myself doing in this situation?' And you're unlikely to see your best self slamming doors or screaming at people you love."[43]

> *This is not new wisdom. Sun Tzu said something similar 2,500 years ago, writing in* The Art of War: *"It is the unemotional, reserved, calm, detached warrior who wins, not the hothead seeking vengeance and not the ambitious seeker of fortune." You don't have to think of your arguments as war, but you can apply the same strategy—not to win your conflicts, but to better sustain your worthwhile relationships.*

More Tips for Managing Relationships

Remember that relationship management is part of any effective emotional intelligence strategy. The Greek philosopher Aristotle put it this way: "Anyone can become angry—that is easy. But to be angry with the right person, to the right degree, at the right time, for the right purpose, and in the right way, this is not easy." It may not be easy, but it is worthwhile.

Here are some additional tips that may help you better manage your relationships. If you see some repetition from previous chapters, that is intentional. The more you hear and learn about these strategies, the more likely you are to practice them and to make them long-lasting habits in your life:

- Be accessible.

- Be interested in other people.

- Practice being transparent in your communication.

- Take your natural style of communication and work at making it even better.

- Make sure your body language matches your tone of voice and that your words match both.

- Make sure that what you say matches what you mean.

- Learn to take constructive feedback.

- Give feedback, but make sure it is helpful and honest.

- Be purposeful in your anger.

- Be actively transparent about what you have decided and why.

- Tackle your problems rather than avoiding them.

- Never avoid a difficult discussion; deal with each issue that arises as soon as possible.

- Work at building trust. It sometimes takes a long time to build yet can be lost in moments.

- When communication is breaking down, suggest a way to fix things, even if it's just to acknowledge the other person's feelings.

- Don't ignore other people's feelings.

- Remember that small gestures matter, such as sending a card or saying "thank you."

- Show appreciation and care as often as possible.

Bradberry and Greaves offer one more piece of advice: "Remember, relationship management is about making choices and acting with the goal of creating an honest deep connection with others." [44]

Check your anger self-awareness on the next page.

EXERCISE – CHAPTER 7

INCREASING YOUR SELF-AWARENESS

1. Recall a recent incidence of anger, then answer the following questions about it:

   a. Were you reactive, or did you take the time to pause and think?

   _____
   _____
   _____
   _____
   _____

   b. When you became angry, did you try to calm your partner—or yourself?

   _____
   _____
   _____
   _____
   _____

   c. Did you attempt to control your partner with your anger?

   _____
   _____
   _____
   _____
   _____

   d. Did a difference of opinion spark the conflict—or your reaction to it?

   _____
   _____
   _____
   _____
   _____

2. What does this anger incident tell you about yourself?

   _____
   _____
   _____
   _____
   _____

3. Was how you responded helpful? If so, in what way was it helpful? If not, in what way was it not helpful?

   _____
   _____
   _____
   _____
   _____

4. Did this anger incident negatively impact one of your relationships? If so, how might you have handled it more productively?

   _____
   _____
   _____
   _____
   _____

> *Conflict is a result of differing opinions.*
> *It is not intended to divide.*
>
> – MARIA L. VEGA

CHAPTER 8
Managing Conflict

Author and speaker Max Lucado once said, "Conflict is inevitable; combat is optional." The nugget of truth in that quotation is that disagreements are a natural part of life, but we also have a choice about how to handle conflict when we must face it. And we all will face it at some point—not only in our personal relationships, but at work as well.

But before we get into strategies for how to handle conflict, it will be helpful to first understand what causes it.

The Origins of Human Conflict

We may think of conflict arising simply because people become angry at one another, but there are deeper issues to examine. According to conflict management experts Carston DeDreu and Michelle Gelfand, there are several root causes of conflict for personal relationships and work teams alike:

1. Conflict over resources.

2. Conflict that comes from threats to self-esteem.

3. Conflict that comes from interruptions to the need for belonging.

4. Conflict due to differences in ideologies and values.

5. Conflict due to differences in understanding.[45]

Conflicts over resources often occur because what is in your best interest may not be in the best interest of the other party; in fact, what may be in your self-interest may actually hurt someone else, and that person often responds accordingly. These conflicts can also lead to or may result from misunderstandings and incomplete information about the circumstances that led to your difference in opinion.

Business consultant and bestselling author Cy Wakeman suggests that conflict, specifically in the workplace, occurs most often not because of personality clashes between coworkers or because of incompetent employees, but because of a lack of clarity.

In other words, conflicts occur primarily because of a failure to communicate clearly. It would be fair to say this is also true for personal relationships. At work, lack of clarity about goals (direction), roles (behavior), and procedures tends to produce the most conflict.

Wakeman also argues that another source of conflict is internal: "A great deal of the conflict we encounter is manufactured in our own minds. When faced with conflict, we tend to quickly move from the bare facts of the situation and create our own mental story that portrays us as helpless victims."[46] That means that your understanding of and attitudes about conflict are also important.

A good relationship starts with you.

Sources of Conflict in Personal Relationships

Disagreements occur in all close relationships. Conflict does not mean that your relationship is a failure. Neither does conflict mean that you can't be happy together. Some examples of the root causes of conflict in personal relationships include:

- **Selfishness** – This occurs when someone in the relationship fails to think of the other person when making decisions.

- **Communication** – Too often, communicating in a relationship leads to an argument. This can occur even when the conflict is over the other person's tone of voice or when anger has been simmering over time.

- <u>Resentment</u> – When one of the partners offends the other, but the hurt is not communicated, neglected emotions may develop into resentment. One person may become distant, causing the other to feel his/her partner is no longer interested in the relationship.

- <u>Finger-Pointing and Criticism</u> – Sometimes in relationships, one partner criticizes the other about everything that goes wrong then claims responsibility when things go right.

- <u>Unrealistic or Distorted Expectations</u> – Many relationships have conflicts because one or both individuals feel that their expectations are not being met. Unfortunately, these expectations are often unrealistic and distorted.

Understanding how conflict arises, its origins and causes, can help you keep perspective as you seek to manage what is an unavoidable and perhaps even necessary part of life.

The Benefits of Healthy Conflict

We all understand that conflict can cause problems for individuals, personal relationships, and teams at work. Unrestrained conflict can result in high levels of stress in the individual, rifts in personal relationships, and ineffective work teams that cannot seem to get the job done.

At work, the danger is that conflict can damage team morale, causing lost productivity, absenteeism, and even mental health issues, which can in turn lead to a reduction in company earnings and profits.[47]

But there are benefits to conflict too—when it's done correctly.

When conflict happens, it's usually noticed. Sometimes people get loud in their anger. Sometimes they withdraw and walk off in a huff. But because conflict gets noticed, it can be a way of recognizing underlying issues that have not been addressed.

Human services researcher and educator Barbara Benoliel says that conflict "can be a motivator that generates new ideas and innovation as well as leads to increased flexibility and a better understanding of working relationships."[48]

This is true even when it is a small minority vocalizing an unpopular opinion or when someone is playing devil's advocate. Those stances may be seen as annoying, contradictory, and even counterproductive.

But sometimes when that occurs, a couple or a group will take the time to reexamine their fundamental assumptions, seek out new information, and be willing to look at the situation from new perspectives. And that can result in more effective results on an individual, interpersonal, or group level.[49]

Furthermore, conflict can also be of benefit to your close personal relationships —when it is understood. When you know the source of your anger, you are less likely to become defensive. That defensiveness can create conflict and often can lead to a fight with your partner. Couples who treat each other with respect and empathy are more apt to live in harmony than those who are prone to sarcasm and harsh language.

Relationships can grow and mature through conflict. It is important, however, to look for the root cause of the problem rather than focusing on surface issues. For your own peace of mind, remember that all relationships have disagreements. Conflict does not mean your relationship is a failure, and healthy relationships grow and mature *through* conflict.

What Does Healthy Conflict Look Like?

People who engage in the kind of conflict that makes work teams and personal relationships thrive are not afraid to put scary topics on the table for discussion. At work, that often makes for lively and interesting meetings, but it also helps teams to solve problems more quickly.

Team management expert Patrick Lencioni puts it this way, "Every effective team I've ever observed had a substantial level of debate."[50] Research shows that conflict can drive change for individuals, teams, and even organizations.[51]

When there are substantial differences of opinion, those who engage in healthy conflict discuss ideas while avoiding personal attacks. That does not mean they are

unemotional—people may express their frustration and their passion for the subject at hand, but that does not necessarily make such discussions chaotic.

If the understood purpose of the conflict is to come to the optimum solution in the shortest timeframe, open and frank discussions are often the best means of accomplishing that goal.

Another aspect of healthy conflict is to ensure that all members of the group are heard and at minimum feel understood. Not everyone will get their own way, but including all opinions creates greater buy-in to the final outcome.[52]

Conflict is also healthy when two people are in a committed personal relationship. Without occasional conflict, the possibility exists that one or both partners are not being transparent. You both have the right to view things differently and to express a difference of opinion without hurting the other person. If people are being honest in voicing an opinion, they can then work together on finding common ground.

Yet in order to reach agreement or compromise and ultimately achieve your goals, whether in a personal relationship or in an organization, conflict needs to be effectively managed.

Strategies for Managing Conflict

It's completely normal, and even healthy, to become angry sometimes. It means you're human. Yet anger resulting in conflict can undermine relationships.

Preventing all anger and conflict is an impossible goal. Instead, on our road toward a better understanding of what makes our anger "tick," we can learn better ways of avoiding negative reactions (such as aggression), while at the same time developing healthy new habits.

Following are several steps you can take toward a healthier way of managing conflict—either in personal relationships or at work.

Step No. 1: Identify your triggers.

Let's revisit an idea from Chapter 2. Some events make us angry. Certain words may push our buttons. These sensitive areas are usually the result of long-standing issues.

In addition to circumstances in the here and now, we may also be clinging to the memory of a past event that made us angry. It helps to keep in mind the events and words that may trigger us; recognizing them may help us know when to pause and reevaluate in the midst of conflict—rather than simply reacting.

What tends to push your buttons?

_____

_____

_____

_____

Step No. 2: Identify the problem.

Have a discussion with your partner or coworker(s) aimed at understanding both sides of an issue. Discuss your needs and the preferred outcomes. Clarify exactly what the conflict or problem involves. In this step, you state what you want and listen to what your partner wants. The goal is for each of you to be able to clearly restate what the other person wants. During your discussion, be sure to use "I" messages and steer clear of blaming the other person.

Write down the results of your discussion. What do you want? What does your partner want? Did you decide on a mutually acceptable goal? If so, what is it?

_____

_____

_____

_____

Step No. 3: Generate several possible solutions.

This is the brainstorming approach. Drawing from a position of mutual agreement, identify your shared goals and interests. Look for alternatives that might solve the problem. Avoid evaluating or judging each idea until all ideas have been suggested.

In this step, you just write them down:

_____

_____

_____

_____

_____

Step No. 4: Consider and evaluate each suggested solution.

Eliminate those ideas that are not acceptable to either of you. Keep narrowing down the ideas until you arrive at one or two that are acceptable to both of you.

At this stage, it important to be honest and use "I" statements to say things like "I would be happy with that" or "I don't think that would be fair to me." Write out two possible solutions:

_____

_____

_____

_____

_____

Step No. 5: Decide on the best solution and select an alternative that is acceptable to both of you.

Make certain that your decision is mutually acceptable. Include an acceptable alternative if your first choice does not work out.

Write out your solution and indicate whether both parties have agreed to it:

_____

_____

_____

_____

Step No. 6: Implement the solution.

It may be necessary to talk about how your solution will be implemented, the timeframe it may take for implementation, and who will be responsible for carrying it out.

Write down the results of your discussion:

_____

_____

_____

_____

Step No. 7: Conduct a follow-up review to determine whether the solution is working as well as you hoped.

Make it a practice to ask your partner how the solution is working and how they feel about it. This will help ascertain whether something was overlooked, misjudged, or if something unexpected may have occurred. Both parties should agree that decisions are always open for revision, yet any modifications should be mutually agreed upon. Write out your observations:

_____

_____

_____

_____

Additional Practices for Effective Conflict Resolution

1. When conflicts erupt, it is important to remain calm. Approach the situation with reason and assertiveness.

2. If necessary, separate yourself from the situation. If you are angry, take time to cool off before communicating.

3. Attack the problem, not the person. Focus on the issue, not your position on the issue. Try starting with a compliment.

4. Communicate your feelings assertively, not aggressively.

5. Work to develop mutual trust.

6. Accept and respect that individual opinions may differ. Work to develop common agreement. Do not try to force compliance.

7. Always keep in mind that diversity of perspective is an advantage that often leads to a better outcome.

8. Do not view the situation as a competition. Work toward a win-win outcome that allows both parties to have some of their needs met.

9. Instead of focusing on areas of opposition and disagreement, concentrate on areas of agreement and common interest.

10. Never jump to conclusions or make assumptions about what another person is feeling or thinking. Ask.

11. Listen without interrupting. Ask for feedback if needed to ensure a clear understanding of the issue.

12. Remember: When only one person's needs are met in a conflict, the matter is NOT resolved, and the conflict will continue.

13. Work at building "power with" rather than "power over" others.

14. Thank the person for listening.

15. Use your emotional intelligence skills. Be aware of your own reactions and manage them effectively. Take time to read the room—checking the "emotional temperature" of the situation—and be ready to manage your relationships.

16. Keep perspective. Remember that "this too shall pass."

Check your conflict resolution skills on the next page.

EXERCISE – CHAPTER 8

CONFLICT RESOLUTION SCENARIOS

Instructions: *Above is a "Conflict Response Wheel" showing a set of easy-to-remember immediate actions you can take when you experience conflict. Below are two conflict scenarios. Read each and, using the wheel above, choose a quick response (or responses) to address that conflict. Explain why you chose that response, how you would implement it, and your expected result.*

Scenario No. 1 (Work): Your new coworker, Gina, asked you for help on a project, but you had to refuse because you were working on another project and had to meet a strict deadline. She hasn't been friendly with you since. Now you need her help on a new project, but she has not responded to your voicemails or emails. How do you overcome this conflict?

_____

_____

_____

_____

_____

_____

Scenario No. 2 (Personal): James and Ramila are looking for their first home together. They both have multiple items on their wish list but have realized they each have a primary concern. James is most concerned about location, Ramila with the price of the home. They have not yet been able to come to an agreement and have come close to giving up their search. How do they overcome this conflict? Are there any other considerations they should take into account?

_____

_____

_____

_____

_____

_____

> *Anger can be an indicator that
> our values are being violated.*
>
> – MARIA L. VEGA

CHAPTER 9

Identifying Your Life Values

One of the guideposts on your road to understanding anger is knowing your values. Your values in life influence your thoughts, feelings, behavior, and how you evaluate yourself and others. Values are the standards by which you measure success and failure.

For example, if you value financial prosperity, you might believe that you should do whatever is necessary to accumulate wealth. Or if you value concern for others, you might consider volunteering your time to help a cause that you believe will benefit society.

Your system of values develops and grows as you begin to recognize, prioritize, and apply your values to your life and your choices.

How Values Influence Your Decision-Making and Your Relationships

According to the Life Values Inventory, values affect how you make decisions about your career, your relationships, your family, your lifestyle, and more. Because your values affect so many vital aspects of your life, it isn't surprising that they influence the choices you make every day.[53]

Specifically, there are two values that carry more weight in how you make decisions that can significantly impact your relationships: **independence** and **interdependence**.

In all relationships, there is a certain amount of tension between independence and interdependence. People need each other not just for survival but in order to thrive emotionally, and yet we each also need some space to be individuals and make independent decisions.

If you place a stronger value on independence, you may put less emphasis on what your partner or colleagues think and do. Instead, you are more likely to place more value on your own thoughts and opinions. By contrast, others may place considerable value on interdependence. In that case, you may choose relationships over independence. You may place more emphasis on the feelings of family and friends and value their opinions as highly or even more highly than your own when making decisions.

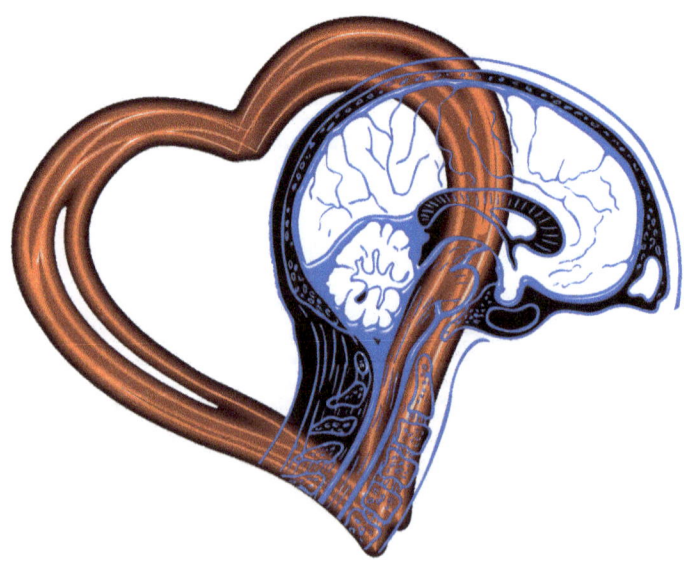

How you value independence and interdependence will directly influence your relationships. For example, a more interdependent spouse may have a greater need for information and a need to be involved in the decision-making process in the relationship. Yet an independent person would be completely okay with their partner making decisions on behalf of the relationship, household, or finances. In fact, the independent person prefers it.

If you are the independent type, your partner's interdependence may come across as needy. If you are the interdependent type, your partner's independence may come across as selfish. Knowing this can help you to reframe your understanding of your partner as you interact.

> *The goal is to be self-aware about what we value and understand how it impacts and influences our relationships. The aim is not to change your independence or interdependence but rather to understand and adjust it according to the needs of your relationship. This further requires the acquisition of effective communication skills so that both partners can understand each other well.*

Awareness of your values and those of your partner can only strengthen your relationship. Becoming more self-aware makes you better at identifying any unmet needs you may have, which can boost your ability to be more assertive and communicate more clearly.[54]

For example, one partner in a relationship may be motivated by a strong need to pursue an ever-increasing income, a desire influenced by some difficult childhood experiences. No amount of wealth accumulation seems to make them feel secure. Their partner could work at understanding that need and make peace with it, recognizing that they share and support the same value—financial security—though to a different extent and for different reasons. A resolution would require communication from both partners in order to first understand one another's needs, then to discover where their values intersect, and finally to negotiate how they will pursue and handle money and the time it takes to acquire it.

In addition to impacting your relationships, knowing your life values also has other benefits. Identifying and thinking about your values can reduce stress, and as we have already learned, reducing stress plays a significant role in understanding and managing anger. Having a deeper understanding of your values can also improve problem-solving and increase life and relationship satisfaction, because you are living up to your values, a.k.a. belief system.

In fact, stress increases when there is disagreement between your choices and your values. In order to truly thrive, it is important that your activities and your values are in alignment. Whether you are at school, at work, at home, or in the community—whether acting alone or within the context of a relationship—you can feel off balance and stressed when your daily activities do not match what you value most. That makes it vital to both define and prioritize your life values.[55]

Recognizing Contradictory Values

In addition to a mismatch between actions and values, you can also experience conflict between two values you hold simultaneously. It is possible to have two primary values, for example, where you have prioritized one over the other so that one closely held value is not being satisfied.

For example, let's say you place a high value on earning income through your business. Another value you hold dearly is to volunteer your time in charitable organizations as a way of giving back to your community. A conflict in values occurs when your business suddenly demands almost all of your time, and you are not able to spend time volunteering for an extended period. Another example is if

you are someone who values your independence, but you suddenly must conform to a group norm that you do not agree with.

Such conflicts in values can create inner stress and discomfort. This can result in something called *cognitive dissonance*.[56]

According to Life Values Inventory, "When there is a conflict between your values, you must carefully consider which values are most important to you."[57]

> *"Cognitive dissonance is [a] phenomenon whereby we have a natural drive for consistency, in that our belief system must be consistent with itself and it must be consistent with our actions . . . But that consistency doesn't always happen, and distress can arise as a result."*
> — Everyday Health

Moreover, what happens when you discover that you are in a marriage or even a work relationship where you and the other person have competing values? People often end up showing disapproval of the other person, feel dissatisfied, and the result is, of course, conflict. The situation can be further aggravated when we feel our values are being criticized or when we feel someone wants to keep us from living out our values in daily life.

An additional factor is that most people fulfill multiple roles in life within their jobs, their primary relationships, as parents, and more. Sometimes these roles create competing interests or require us to live out competing values. The result can be growing feelings of frustration and resentment and a general feeling of dissatisfaction with life. And that can threaten and even damage your personal relationships.

Determining Your Values

So that you can effectively determine whether there are conflicts between the values that you hold within or those between you and someone with whom you have a close relationship, you should take some time to think through and assess your values and that of your partner (or what you would like in a future partner).

Knowing what your strongest values are can also help you determine your greatest stressors and assist you in developing goals, both for yourself and in your relationships.

At the end of this chapter you will take a quick self-assessment that will help you determine your top values. The same assessment can be completed with a partner so that you can determine the primary values you have in common.

There are also many other ways of determining your personal and relationship values. For example, R. Kelly Crace, PhD, and Duane Brown, PhD, of Applied Psychology Resources, Inc., created the Life Values Inventory consisting of fourteen values that measure the characteristics of people who hold a particular value, potential stressors associated with that value, and how that value may interact with other values.

Those values are: achievement, belonging, concern for the environment, concern for others, creativity, financial prosperity, health and activity, humility, independence, interdependence, objective analysis, responsibility, privacy, and spirituality.[58]

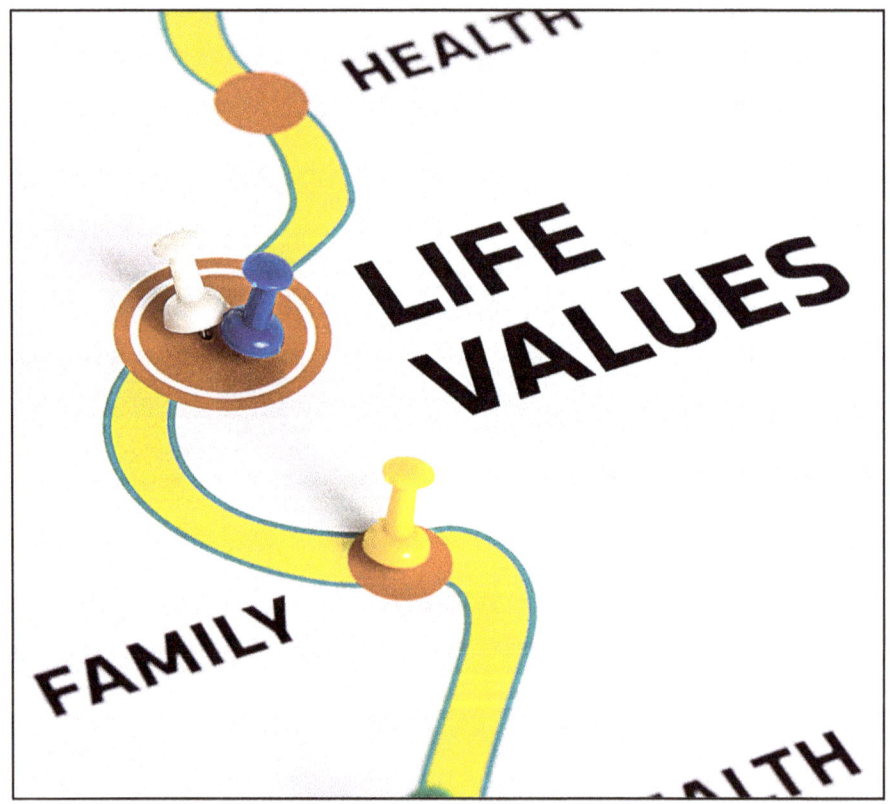

Another way of assessing your values is to take the VIA Survey of Character Strengths. Although technically not a values assessment, it does give people an idea of the characteristics that are most important to them in terms of their personal strengths, which are very similar to a list of values.

The characteristics measured by the VIA survey are:

- Appreciation of beauty and excellence
- Bravery
- Creativity
- Curiosity
- Fairness
- Forgiveness
- Gratitude
- Honesty
- Hope
- Humility
- Humor
- Judgment
- Kindness
- Leadership
- Love of learning
- Love
- Perspective
- Prudence
- Self-regulation
- Social intelligence
- Spirituality
- Teamwork
- Zest[59]

Both of these assessments are readily available through an Internet search and can be taken without cost. It may be useful to conduct more than one assessment of your values, as each may give you different ideas about what is most important to you.

> *Check your values via the assessment starting on the next page.*

EXERCISE – CHAPTER 9

CHECK YOUR VALUES

This exercise is intended as yet another way to monitor your "check engine light." It will help you determine your strongest values for your career, your relationships, your decision making—for all aspects of your life.

<u>Instructions</u>: *You will need the Values Inventory sheet on the next page and a pencil or pen.*

1. *Read the list of values on the following page and put a check mark by any value that speaks to you. You may write in a value if you don't see it on the list.*

2. *Next, take a few minutes to narrow down your choices to your top ten values by placing an X next to them.*

3. *Now, narrow your choices to your top five values. Circle them.*

   All of the values you checked off are meaningful to you and influence your behavior, but focus on your top five for the purpose of this assignment, as they will give you insight into your decision making and help you learn more about what is important to you.

VALUES INVENTORY

	Achievement		Family		Patience
	Advancement		Fast-paced Living		Peace
	Adventure		Fast-paced Work		Persistence
	Affection		Fitness		Personal Growth
	Appreciation		Forgiveness		Physical Challenges
	Art (the Arts)		Free Time		Pleasure
	Autonomy		Freedom		Poise
	Balance		Friendship		Popularity
	Beauty		Fun		Power/Authority
	Belonging		Generosity		Privacy
	Boldness		Gratitude		Professionalism
	Caring		Happiness		Promotion
	Challenge		Health		Prosperity
	Clarity		Helping People		Public Service
	Communication		Home		Purity
	Community		Honesty		Quality
	Compassion		Humor		Quality Relationships
	Competition		Inclusion		Reciprocity
	Contentment		Independence		Recognition
	Cooperation		Influence		Reputation
	Courage		Inner Harmony		Responsibility
	Creativity		Integrity		Security
	Curiosity		Intellectual Prestige		Self-Respect
	Decisiveness		Intelligence		Serenity
	Democracy		Invention		Service
	Determination		Involvement		Sophistication
	Diversity		Job Satisfaction		Stability
	Ecology		Justice		Status
	Economic Security		Kindness		Strength
	Effectiveness		Knowledge		Success
	Efficiency		Learning		Supervisory Work Role
	Encouragement		Location		Teamwork
	Endurance		Love		Time Alone
	Entrepreneurialism		Loyalty		Trust/Trustworthiness
	Ethics		Meaningful Work		Truth
	Excellence		Merit		Variety/Change
	Excitement		Money		Wealth/Financial Gain
	Expertise		Nature		Willingness
	Fairness		Openness		Wisdom
	Faith/Religion		Optimism		
	Fame		Order		

List your top five values here along with what each means to you. For example, if you list faith/religion, is it a primary value because you believe all other values are based on it, or is it because you want to belong to a community of like-minded believers, or something else?

1. _____

_____

_____

_____

2. _____

_____

_____

_____

3. _____

_____

_____

_____

4. _____

_____

_____

_____

5. _____

_____

_____

_____

Hold onto your values list. In the next chapter you can refer to it as you determine your mission statement.

> *Don't let anger become HOME.*
> – MARIA L. VEGA

CHAPTER 10
Roadmap to Managing Your Emotions

One of the ways you can look at managing emotions, specifically anger, is to regard heading toward your goal—greater self-control—as if you are using a roadmap.

Follow what you have learned, use the directions, and one day not too far in the future you will arrive at each guidepost, one step at a time, until you reach your final destination: self-management of your emotions, specifically within the context of your personal or work relationships.

In this chapter we'll revisit some of the things we've already learned in this workbook and learn a few new things along the way:

- **Guidepost No. 1** (on your roadmap toward healthier relationships) is to identify the needs you have in a particular relationship, whether current or future.

- **Guidepost No. 2** is to identify your triggers.

- **Guidepost No. 3**. is to recognize and understand stress.

- **Guidepost No. 4** is to identify your style of communication.

- **Guidepost No. 5** is to identify your values.

- **Guidepost No. 6** is to create a Relationship Mission Statement that will help you understand yourself better and help you understand the values and goals you have for your relationship (your current one or one you may be seeking).

Guidepost No. 1: Identify Your Needs

The road to Guidepost No. 1 is to identify the important needs you have for a relationship (current or future). Then, once you identify them, in your own words define each one, describing what that need means to you.

If your need is love, for example, the word "love" may have various meanings to different people. But what do *you* mean by love? You may mean love that is transparent, honest, and committed.

So your first need in a relationship is the "need to have love that is transparent, committed, and honest." (That describes love for you and what you need when you use the word "love.")

Write down three needs you have for a relationship. Be sure to define your meanings carefully:

1. _____

_____

_____

2. _____

_____

_____

3. _____

_____

Guidepost No. 2: Identify Your Triggers

Triggers are situations, interactions, or personality traits that set us off, usually resulting in an uncontrollable emotion, such as anger, fear, or hurt.

Triggers access the part of the brain that stores data. When triggered, you are most likely to feel the emotion that was connected to a root cause or experience.

Identifying your triggers is important; once you become aware of them, you can better judge how to respond. For example, you can choose to stay away from conversations or situations that may potentially set off the trigger.

Refer back to the exercises you completed in Chapter 2 when you identified your personal triggers.

Then write down three triggers that could potentially affect your current (or future) relationship. In order to increase your self-awareness, also identify and write down the root cause for each:

1. _____

_____

_____

2. _____

_____

_____

3. _____

_____

_____

Guidepost No. 3: Identify Your Stressors

In Chapter 3 we learned what stress does to you physically, emotionally, and behaviorally. We also learned that stress is a mismatch between a demand and the resources you have available to meet that demand.

Stress is a natural response our body experiences when life gets too hectic, or when we forget to recharge or ask for help.

Stress can cause three different types of changes:

1. Physical changes in your body.

2. Behavioral changes, including to your personality.

3. Emotional changes.

Identifying what stress does to you in each of those areas will not only help you understand the main stressors in your life, but will also help you ask for what you need and assist you in creating a plan that will help you to avoid stress as much as possible. It will also help you avoid conflict with others, including in your primary relationships.

Write down your main relationship stressors:

_____

_____

_____

_____

_____

Guidepost No. 4: Identify Your Communication Style

Remember the four styles of communication discussed in Chapter 6? (Passive, Passive-Aggressive, Aggressive, and Assertive.) We are likely to navigate through all of them at one time or another, but one style is typically dominant.

Identifying what style you use most often is the beginning of understanding the dynamics of your relationships and how your communication style may be influencing them.

Becoming aware of your communication style and that of your partner will allow you to make adjustments in the way you communicate and in the way you seek to understand the other person.

Based on your understanding of communication styles from Chapter 6, identify and write down your primary communication style.

What are some ways in which your style of communication may contribute to successful outcomes for a relationship you currently have or one you may be seeking? Unsuccessful outcomes?

_____

_____

_____

_____

_____

Guidepost No. 5: Identify Your Values

Values are the lenses through which you view yourself and the world. They are the basis for your thoughts, feelings, and behavior.

The road to Guidepost No. 5 is to identify the top three values that will make you feel satisfied in your relationships. For example, yours might be *achievement*, *independence*, and *responsibility*.

Once you have identified your top three values, in your own words define what they mean to you. For example, responsibility might mean "being ethical, honest, and reliable," and achievement might mean being able to retire by age fifty with the means to travel the world.

Write down three values for your current or future relationship. You may want to refer back to the exercises you completed in Chapter 9 when you identified your personal and relationship values. Be sure to define your meanings carefully:

1. _____

_____

_____

2. _____

_____

_____

3. _____

_____

_____

Guidepost No. 6: Create Your Relationship Mission Statement

Once you come to understand your needs and values you can begin to apply the principles you have learned here and formulate a plan of action. One of the ways you can do that is to create a mission statement.

Therefore, to reach this guidepost you will work to create a relationship mission statement addressing one of your relationships. This mission statement can be a valuable tool in crystalizing what is important to you and guiding you toward living your life intentionally.

Creating Your Relationship Mission Statement

Research has demonstrated repeatedly that when clear goals are associated with learning, your brain is much more effective at gaining knowledge.[31] With that in mind, you should review the goals you wrote down in Chapter 4, your values from Chapter 9, and your roadmap answers in this chapter, and begin to create a mission statement for a significant relationship (either current or future).

> *Keep an eye on your check engine light by creating a mission statement, starting on the next page.*

EXERCISE – CHAPTER 10

CREATE A RELATIONSHIP MISSION STATEMENT

We all want love, companionship, friendship, and commitment, but to truly have a successful relationship you must first identify what that relationship means to you, what the goals of the relationship are, where you see it headed, and the key steps that will support your ongoing respect and love.

Creating a relationship mission statement works whether you create it alone or with a partner. It can be completed for a current relationship or by keeping in mind the type of relationship you desire in the future.

In all cases, be sure to include all the things that are important to you in a relationship, such as values, needs, leisure activities, children, financial beliefs and goals, current and future goals, or changes in the different stages of your journey together.

If you work with your partner, your relationship mission statement can help you as a couple define the expectations, wants, needs, and goals for your relationship.[60] According to psychologist Susan Orenstein, PhD, a mission statement is a "declaration created and agreed upon by the couple that guides their principles, goals, and values."[61]

Steps to writing your relationship mission statement:

1. List your dreams, goals, and values.

2. List your financial beliefs.

3. List how you would like to spend your leisure time; what activities are important to you?

4. List your plans for retirement.

5. List your future goals.

6. Answer the question: What is my definition of love?

7. Answer the question: How will nurturing and protecting a partner look in my relationship?

There is no word limit to your relationship mission statement, but it is a good idea to keep it to a single page—something that can be displayed within a frame.

EXAMPLE RELATIONSHIP MISSION STATEMENT

Because we both value success and accomplishment, our relationship will be goal-oriented:

1. *We will attentively share our goals and vision with each other.*
2. *We will both be driven but also be aware of each other's needs.*
3. *We will give each other space but will be warm and loving at the end of the day.*
4. *We will celebrate each other's success and be supportive every step of the way.*
5. *Our plans and goals will always meet at the end of the road for the well-being of our relationship.*
6. *We will be each other's best friend and shoulder to lay on.*
7. *We will always keep the communication flowing, even when it becomes challenging.*
8. *We will always keep laughter, fun, and excitement at the forefront of our goals.*
9. *All of our accomplishments will be shared and will become one.*

Because we are human, we will fail at some of these things from time to time. However, when that happens, because we are friends, one will pick up the slack for the other until we are both back on track.

WRITE YOUR RELATIONSHIP MISSION STATEMENT HERE:

The Final Step: Purchase a nice frame for your mission statement, print it in an attractive font, and place it in your home just as a business proudly displays its mission statement to remind its employees of the purpose and goals that will drive the culture and success of the organization. Your Relationship Mission Statement serves the same purpose for either a current or future relationship.[62]

Congratulations!

You have successfully completed your roadmap to understanding anger.

NOTES

[1] This was especially true during the 2020 coronavirus pandemic. Harter, J., & Gandhi, V. (2021, June 15). *7 Things We Learned about U.S. and Canadian Employees in 2020*. Gallup. https://www.gallup.com/workplace/350123/united-states-canada-workplace-trends.aspx

[2] Novaco, R. W. (2000). Anger. In A. E. Kazdin (Ed.), *Encyclopedia of Psychology: 8 Volume Set, 1*. American Psychological Association.

[3] Long, N. J., Long, J. E., & Whitson, S. (2008). T*he Angry Smile: The Psychology of Passive-Aggressive Behavior in Families, Schools, and Workplaces* (2nd ed). Pro Ed.

[4] Booth, J., Ireland, J., Mann, S., Eslea, M., & Holyoak, L. (2017). Anger Expression and Suppression at Work: Causes, Characteristics, and Predictors. *International Journal of Conflict Management, 28*(3), 368–382.; Cristiano, S. (2020). Suppressed Anger and Response to Facial Expressions of Emotion. *Dissertation Abstracts International: Section B: The Sciences and Engineering, 81*(5-B).; Sullivan, S., & Kahn, J. H. (2019). Individual Differences in Expressive Suppression and the Subjective Experience, Verbal Disclosure, and Behavioral Expression of Anger. *Personality and Individual Differences*. Advance online publication.

[5] Golden, B. (2020, July 23). *Displaced Anger: One Destructive Way We Disavow Anger*. Psychology Today. https://www.psychologytoday.com/us/blog/overcoming-destructive-anger/202007/displaced-anger-one-destructive-way-we-disavow-anger

[6] Artz, N., & Westphalen, D. (2021, January 28). *Repressed Anger: Signs, Causes, Treatments, & 8 Ways to Cope*. Choosing Therapy. https://www.choosingtherapy.com/repressed-anger/

[7] Anthony. (2010, February 12). *Stressor vs. Trigger - What Is A Trigger?* MyPTSD. https://www.myptsd.com/threads/stressor-vs-trigger-what-is-a-trigger.13912/; Cuncic, A. (2020, December 3). *What Does It Mean to Be 'Triggered': Types of Triggering Events and Coping Strategies*. VeryWellMind. https://www.verywellmind.com/what-does-it-mean-to-be-triggered-4175432

[8] Brown, T. M., & Fee, E. (2002, October). Walter Bradford Cannon: Pioneer Physiologist of Human Emotions. *American Journal of Public Health, 92*(10), 1594–1595.

[9] Seladi-Schulman, J. (2018, July 23). *What Part of the Brain Controls Emotions?* Healthline. https://www.healthline.com/health/what-part-of-the-brain-controls-emotions

[10] Villines, Z. (2019, March 16). *6 Ways the Limbic System Impacts Physical, Emotional, and Mental Health*. Goodtherapy.org. https://www.goodtherapy.org/blog/6-ways-the-limbic-system-impacts-physical-emotional-and-mental-health-0316197

[11] Mayo Clinic. (2021, July 8). *Chronic Stress Puts Your Health at Risk*. https://www.mayoclinic.org/healthy-lifestyle/stress-management/in-depth/stress/art-20046037

[12] Mind.org. (n.d.). *How to Cope with Anger*. https://www.mind.org.uk/information-support/types-of-mental-health-problems/anger/causes-of-anger/

[13] Tartakovsky, M. (2019, September 14). *How to Empower Yourself When You Feel Powerless and Helpless*. PsychCentral. https://psychcentral.com/blog/how-to-empower-yourself-when-you-feel-powerless-and-helpless#1

[14] This quote has been attributed to various people, but the first written occurrence was attributed to Charles Eads. Phelan, M. (2019, September 17). *The History of "Hurt People Hurt People."* Slate. https://slate.com/culture/2019/09/hurt-people-hurt-people-quote-origin-hustlers-phrase.html

[15] de Castella, T. (2013, April 23). *Luis Suarez: Does Anger Management Actually Work?* BBC. https://www.bbc.com/news/magazine-22264123

[16] Bhandari, S. (2020, November 17). *What Does Stress Do to the Body?* WebMD. https://www.webmd.com/balance/stress-management/stress-and-the-body

[17] Bhandari, S. (2020, November 16). *Is My Stress Level Too High?* WebMD. https://www.webmd.com/balance/stress-management/stress-level-too-high

[18] Gardner, S. S. (2020, November 4). *How to Quiet Your Mind*. WebMD. https://www.webmd.com/balance/ss/slideshow-how-to-quiet-mind

[19] American Psychological Association. (2014, July 1). *Coping with Stress at Work*. https://www.apa.org/topics/healthy-workplaces/work-stress

[20] Sorgen, C. (2006, April 6). *Anger Management: Counting to 10 and Beyond*. WebMD. https://www.webmd.com/sex-relationships/features/anger-management-counting-to-ten

[21] National Institutes of Health. (n.d.). *5 Things You Should Know About Stress*. https://www.nimh.nih.gov/health/publications/stress/

[22] Multiple sources were used for the stress assessments, including: Bhandari, *Is My Stress Level Too High?*; Cigna. (2019, April). *The Effects of Stress and Their Impact on Your Health*. https://www.cigna.com/individuals-families/health-wellness/effects-of-stress-and-their-impact-on-your-health; Fazel, F. (n.d.). *Stress Level Test (Self-Assessment)*. PsyCom. https://www.psycom.net/stress-test; PsychCentral. (n.d.). *How Stressed Are You? Stress Test*. https://psychcentral.com/quizzes/stress-test#1; Saladino, L. (2021, April 22). *Are Your Stress Levels Too High? Take This Quiz to Find Out*. Health.com. https://www.health.com/condition/stress/test-your-stress-level; The Greater Good Science Center at the University of California, Berkeley. (n.d.). *Stress and Anxiety Quiz*. https://greatergood.berkeley.edu/quizzes/take_quiz/stress_and_anxiety.

[23] Bradberry, T., & Greaves, J. (2009). *Emotional intelligence 2.0*. TalentSmart.

[24] Anthony, *Stressor vs. Trigger - What Is A Trigger?*; Cuncic, *What Does It Mean to Be 'Triggered'*.

[25] Segal, J., Smith, M., Robinson, L., & Shubin, J. (2021, July). *Improving Emotional Intelligence (EQ)*. Help Guide. https://www.helpguide.org/articles/mental-health/emotional-intelligence-eq.htm#

[26] Thompson, J. (2011, September 30). *Is Nonverbal Communication a Numbers Game?* Psychology Today. https://www.psychologytoday.com/us/blog/beyond-words/201109/is-nonverbal-communication-numbers-game

[27] Coaching Leaders, Ltd. (2007). *Emotional Intelligence Self-Assessment*. https://www.alchemyformanagers.co.uk/index.php?target=content&path=topics/Emotional%20Intelligence/files/EQ%20Self%20Assessment.pdf

[28] Mawhinney, T., & Sagan, L. L. (2007, February). The Power of Personal Relationships. *Phi Beta Kappa, 88*(6), 460–464. https://doi.org/10.1177/003172170708800611

[29] Thompson, *Is Nonverbal Communication a Numbers Game?*

[30] Global Training Institute. (n.d.). *Module Four: Paraverbal Communication Skills*. https://gtionline.edu.au/short_course_repository/Communication_Strategies/pages/index15.html

[31] Wertheim, E. G. (n.d.). *The Importance of Effective Communication*. Northeastern University, College of Business Administration. https://ysrinfo.files.wordpress.com/2012/06/effectivecommunication5.pdf

[32] Meleen, M. (n.d.). *Examples of Body Language: Recognize Nonverbal Cues*. Your Dictionary. https://examples.yourdictionary.com/examples-of-body-language.html

[33] Ohio Employment First. (2019, June 27). *Non-Verbal Communication*. https://ohioemploymentfirst.org/up_doc/Non-VerbalCommunication7232019.pdf

[34] Anderson, D., Stuart, J., Abadi, M. Gal, S. (2019, January 5). *5 Everyday Hand Gestures That Can Get You in Serious Trouble Outside the US*. Business Insider. https://www.businessinsider.com/hand-gestures-offensive-different-countries-2018-6

[35] Ni, P. (2020, October 4). *7 Signs of a Passive-Aggressive Gaslighter*. Psychology Today. https://www.psychologytoday.com/us/blog/communication-success/202010/7-signs-passive-aggressive-gaslighter

[36] Cherry, K. (2020, April 29). *What Is the Negativity Bias?* VeryWellMind. https://www.verywellmind.com/negative-bias-4589618

[37] Bradberry, T., & Greaves, J. (2009). *Emotional intelligence 2.0*. TalentSmart.

[38] Savarese, I. H. (2013, September 19). *Anger in Relationships: Owning Yours, Softening Your Partner's*. Good Therapy. https://www.goodtherapy.org/blog/anger-in-relationships-owning-yours-softening-your-partners-0919134

[39] Smith, K. (2020, November 24). *When Anger Becomes Emotional Abuse: How to Control Anger and Frustration in a Relationship*. PsyCom. https://www.psycom.net/control-anger-frustration-relationship

[40] Bradberry & Greaves, *Emotional Intelligence 2.0*.

[41] Savarese, *Anger in Relationships*.

[42] Smith, *When Anger Becomes Emotional Abuse*.

[43] Ibid.

[44] Bradberry & Greaves, *Emotional Intelligence 2.0*.

[45] DeDreu, C. K. W., & Gelfand, M. J. (2013). *The Psychology of Conflict and Conflict Management in Organizations*. Routledge, Taylor & Francis.

[46] Wakeman, C. (2016, March 17). *5 Tips to End Workplace Conflict Once and For All*. Success. https://www.success.com/5-tips-to-end-workplace-conflict-once-and-for-all/

[47] Benoliel, B. (2017, May 30). *What's Your Conflict Management Style?* WaldenU. https://www.waldenu.edu/news-and-events/walden-news/2017/0530-whats-your-conflict-management-style; Wakeman, *5 Tips to End Workplace Conflict Once and For All*.

[48] Benoliel, *What's Your Conflict Management Style?*

[49] DeDreu & Gelfand, *The Psychology of Conflict and Conflict Management in Organizations*.

[50] Lencioni, P. (2002). *The Five Dysfunctions of a Team*. Jossey-Bass.

[51] DeDreu & Gelfand, *The Psychology of Conflict and Conflict Management in Organizations*.

[52] Lencioni, *The Five Dysfunctions of a Team*.
[53] Life Values Inventory. *Life Values Inventory: Clarifying Your Personal Truth.* https://www.lifevaluesinventory.org/
[54] Selig, M. (2018, November 27). 9 Surprising Superpowers of Knowing Your Core Values. *Psychology Today.* https://www.psychologytoday.com/us/blog/changepower/201811/9-surprising-superpowers-knowing-your-core-values
[55] Life Values Inventory. (2021). *Life Values Inventory: Clarifying Your Personal Truth.*
[56] Lawler, M. (2018, March 6). *What Does Cognitive Dissonance Mean? The Theory and Definition.* Everyday Health. https://www.everydayhealth.com/neurology/cognitive-dissonance/what-does-cognitive-dissonance-mean-theory-definition/
[57] Life Values Inventory. *Life Values Inventory: Clarifying Your Personal Truth.*
[58] Ibid.
[59] VIA Institute on Character. (n.d.). *VIA Character Strengths Survey.* https://www.viacharacter.org
[60] Tartakovsky, M. (2015, May 14). *A Simple Tool for a More Meaningful Relationship.* PsychCentral. https://psychcentral.com/blog/a-simple-tool-for-a-more-meaningful-relationship#1
[61] Moeller, A. J., Theiler, J. M., & Wu, C. (2012). Goal Setting and Student Achievement: A Longitudinal Study. *Modern Language Journal, 96*(2), 153–169.
[62] Tartakovsky, M. (2015, May 14). *A Simple Tool for a More Meaningful Relationship.* Psych Central. https://psychcentral.com/blog/a-simple-tool-for-a-more-meaningful-relationship#1

Image Credits:

All images are used by permission or are in the public domain and copyright free. Compass image by Werner Moser on Pixabay, Check engine image by Deborah Jackson, accentonwords.com. Brain image by OpenClipart-Vectors on Pixabay. Brain network city image by Gerd Altman on Pixabay. Stress pencil image by Pedro Figueras on Pixabay. Stress button image by kalhh on Pixabay. Coffee and book image by Melk Hagelslag on Pixabay. Hand holding social network image by Gerd Altman on Pixabay. Affection image by Free-Photos on Pixabay. Anger image by Devanath on Pixabay. Anxiety image by Damali Conceptuals on Pixabay. Attraction image by Royal Anwar on Pixabay. Danger image by Tobias Heine on Pixabay. Disgust image by Tom Staziker on Pixabay. Fear image by Ria Sopala on Pixabay. Group of people image by sanuas on Pixabay. Happiness image by Pexels on Pixabay. Hostility image by Ryan McGuire on Pixabay. Interest image by Khusen Rustamov on Pixabay. Sadness image by Małgorzata Tomczak on Pixabay. Surprise image by Pezibear on Pixabay. Worry image by Khusen Rustamov on Pixabay. You like me image by Rodrigo Conceicao on Pixabay. Communication image by Gerd Altmann on Pixabay. Family hearts image by Matla Brand on Pixabay. Passive image by Chakrapong Worathat on Pixabay. In your face image by Gerd Altman on Pixabay. Sarcasm image by Alexas_Fotos on Pixabay. Conflict management image from Canva. Relationships composite image by Gerd Altmann & Tumisu on Pixabay. Positivity image by Alfonso Cerezo on Pixabay. Glad you're back image by by Ксения Паскаль on Pixabay. Couple communicating image by Alexandr Podvalny on Pixabay. Values image by Nattanan Kanchanaprat on Pixabay. Heart-brain image by Gerd Altman on Pixabay. Balance scales image by Arek Socha on Pixabay. Life values image from Canva. Pins in a map image by piviso on Pixabay. Frame image by Robert Rizzo on Pixabay.

Cover design by Deborah Jackson, accentonwords.com. Compass image on the cover by Werner Moser on Pixabay,

Thank you all for your beautiful artwork!